I0689558

The British Seashore

First published in 1954, *The British Seashore* is written for those who love to wander along the coast- along the beaches of shingle and sand, the rocky shores, in the salt marshes, and up steep cliff paths. For the coastline of Britain is one of the most varied in the world, not only in its general scenery but also in the many interesting animals and plants which it supports. Fishes, winkles, mussels, starfish, crabs and jellyfish-these are the commonly known animals of the shore, but equally common although not so well known are the sea firs, sea cucumbers, sea squirts and many others- some very beautiful and all worth knowing about. But it is not enough just to know the names of these animals and plants; and in this book much is told of their habits, how they grow and feed, and affect each other 's lives, and of how shellfish, seaweeds and seaside plants are used by man, either for food or for manufacturing purposes. This is a book for general readers interested in seashores.

The British Seashore

H.G. Vevers

Routledge
Taylor & Francis Group

First published in 1954
by Routledge & Kegan Paul Ltd.

This edition first published in 2024 by Routledge
4 Park Square, Milton Park, Abingdon, Oxon, OX14 4RN

and by Routledge
605 Third Avenue, New York, NY 10017

Routledge is an imprint of the Taylor & Francis Group, an informa business

© H.G. Vevers, 1954

Publisher's Note
The publisher has gone to great lengths to ensure the quality of this reprint but points out that some imperfections in the original copies may be apparent.

Disclaimer
The publisher has made every effort to trace copyright holders and welcomes correspondence from those they have been unable to contact.

A Library of Congress record exists under LCCN: 55026968

ISBN: 978-1-032-77612-5 (hbk)
ISBN: 978-1-003-48437-0 (ebk)
ISBN: 978-1-032-77617-0 (pbk)

Book DOI 10.4324/9781003484370

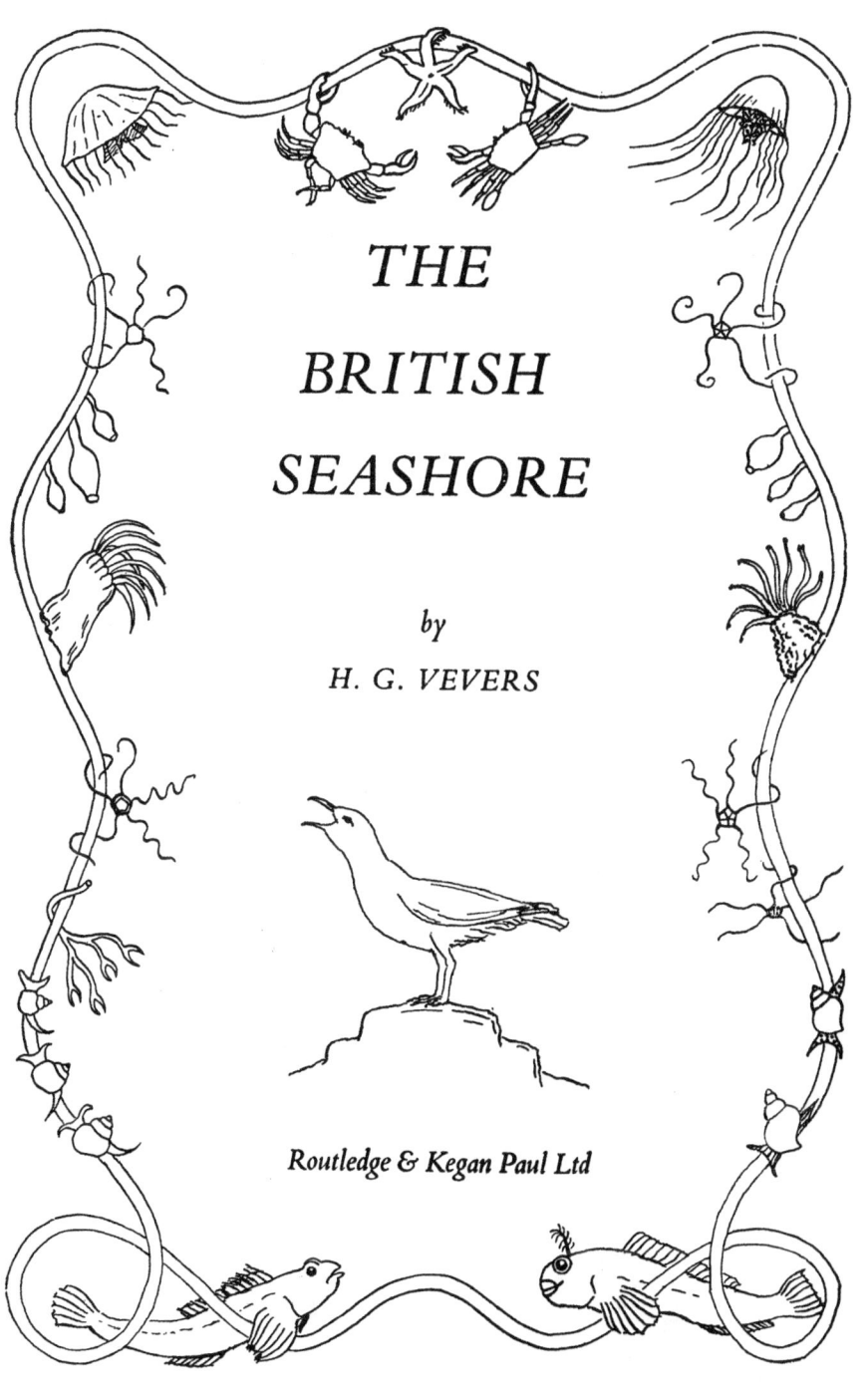

THE
BRITISH
SEASHORE

by

H. G. VEVERS

Routledge & Kegan Paul Ltd

First published in 1954
by Routledge & Kegan Paul Ltd
Broadway House, 68-74 Carter Lane
London E.C.4
Printed in Great Britain
by Latimer Trend & Co Ltd
Plymouth

To

GEOFFREY

Contents

Plates

Introduction

SOME two-thirds of the earth's surface are covered by sea water and yet we know little about the sea compared with what we know about dry land. It is, indeed, only in the last hundred years that we have begun to find out more about the nature of the sea. Before this Man had been satisfied to know how to navigate a ship at sea and how to make a living, even if a poor one, from the fishes and whales of the sea.

In Britain and some other countries the increased leisure of the nineteenth century allowed men to pay more attention to the sea and to the animals and plants living in it. Much of this early work was done on the seashore. In England one of the pioneers was Philip Gosse, who wrote and illustrated many accurate and valuable books on the animals and plants of the shore and coast. It is only in the last few years that his work on sea anemones published in 1860 has been replaced by a more modern book of the same degree of accuracy. Gosse had many followers, among them Charles Kingsley, who wrote *Glaucus, or the Wonders of the Shore* as well as *The Water Babies*.

Britain is fortunate in having one of the most varied coastlines in the world, in fact all types of shore are represented except fringing coral reefs and mangrove swamps which are restricted to warmer waters. It is, however, not only the seashore or beach between tidemarks which holds so much of interest. There is also plenty to be seen and found in the stretch of land above high water—the sand dunes and saltmarshes where maritime conditions give a special and interesting vegetation and

Introduction

the cliffs and offshore islands where many sea birds find food and nest sites.

There is a certain satisfaction in knowing the names of the animals and plants which we see on the shore, and some of the chapters in this book should help the reader to identify them. Once the main animals and plants are known, a walk on the shore or along a strip of sand dune or a cliff path will become increasingly interesting, for one will begin to know what these animals and plants are doing, how they feed, move and reproduce. Some will find that their interest centres on one particular group of animals or perhaps on the fossils embedded in coastal cliffs, and for them there are books, listed at the end, which go into more detail. The main purposes of this book are to increase your enjoyment of the seashore and coast, and to give a background on which you may base further reading and exploration.

1. The Sea and the Shore

Ask me no more: the moon may draw the sea;
The cloud may stoop from heaven and take the shape,
· With fold to fold, of mountain or of cape;
 TENNYSON: 'The Princess'

I F you take a glass of water, put a tablespoonful of ordinary table salt into it and stir, the salt will disappear and dissolve in the water. The water in the glass will then be just as salty as sea water and will taste very like it. But a sea fish could not live in this water, because animals and plants in the sea need other salts as well as common salt (sodium chloride). Sea water contains a number of different salts, of which there is a list on page 139. It has been found that in 1,000 parts of sea water there are as many as 35 parts of salts, and these amounts are about the same in all parts of the sea, except where fresh water from a river runs into the sea. When this happens the water is brackish and is not true sea water. Brackish water is found, not only in river estuaries, but also in rock pools near high-water mark which may be filled with a mixture of rain water and sea water.

The water along the seashore is always on the move, sometimes slowly, sometimes fast. The most obvious of these movements are the tides. Twice a day the tide rises and covers most

B   I

The Sea and the Shore

of the shore giving high tide and twice it falls leaving the shore bare at low tide. There is usually a period of twelve hours and twenty-five minutes between two high tides, and the same applies to low tides. So a high tide at Plymouth will be succeeded by a low tide there about six hours later, and by another high tide twelve hours twenty-five minutes after the first high tide, but high tide does not occur at every place on the coast at the same time. The high tide that strikes Plymouth at midnight will not reach Dover until 6.30 a.m., or London Bridge until 8.20 a.m.

About every two weeks, at full moon and new moon, the tides rise higher and fall lower on the beach than is usual; these are known as *spring tides*, from the Old English word meaning 'to bulge', so that spring tides are those which bulge or rise up higher on the beach. At other times one gets *neap tides*, which have a smaller rise and fall of water. Neap tides occur around the time of half moon.

Spring tides are often called 'big' tides because of the much greater rise and fall of the water which occurs at such times. In Britain the height of the high spring tides is on the average about 16½ feet above the height of the low spring tides. It is difficult to imagine this on a gently sloping beach, but it can easily be seen on a pier or on a steep rock rising out of the sea. This figure of 16½ feet is known as the average range of spring tides, and it is nearly double the average range of the neap tides, which is 8½ feet. In practice, different places along the coasts have different tidal ranges, and in the estuary of the River Severn, below Bristol, the average range of spring tides is about 42 feet, while the range of neaps is only 21 feet. On the other hand, the tidal range on some parts of the Suffolk coast may be no more than 2–3 feet. The greatest tides known are in the Bay of Fundy in eastern Canada, where the maximum tidal range is 53 feet.

The tides come in towards the British Isles from the Atlantic

The Sea and the Shore

Ocean in the form of tidal waves. As these waves approach the land the water begins to pile up, so that in channels, as between France and England, there are bigger tides than out in the ocean. In fact on the shores of islands right out in the ocean you get very small tides. Every time the tide goes out the waters along the shore stream towards the sea. Sometimes these tidal streams are quite fast, especially in narrow channels, where the fast water currents are often very dangerous for bathers. In the English Channel the speed of the tidal stream is about two miles per hour, a very slow walking pace, but in the channel between the Orkney and Shetland Isles the speed is as much as ten miles an hour. Tidal streams such as this move sand and gravel along the shore and can gradually change the shape of the shore.

A knowledge of the tides is quite essential to those who live and work on the sea in Britain. Even small ships cannot enter certain harbours except at high tide. This does not happen to the same extent in the Mediterranean where the rise and fall of the tides is very small. Perhaps this accounts for the trouble experienced by Caesar during his invasion of Britain. It is said that the Roman transport ships drawn up on the beach at Deal and Walmer were lost because the crews did not know about the spring tides which successfully broke them up. Caesar's allies from Gaul, who knew something of the Channel tides, lost none of their ships.

Nowadays calculations of the height to be reached by the tide on a given day are accurate to within a few inches, and this knowledge is of great value, not only for the docking of ocean-going liners but also for military operations like the 1944 invasion of Europe from Britain. Tide predictions work out very well in most cases, but there are times when a strong wind, whether onshore or offshore, will make a great difference to the height of the tide.

3

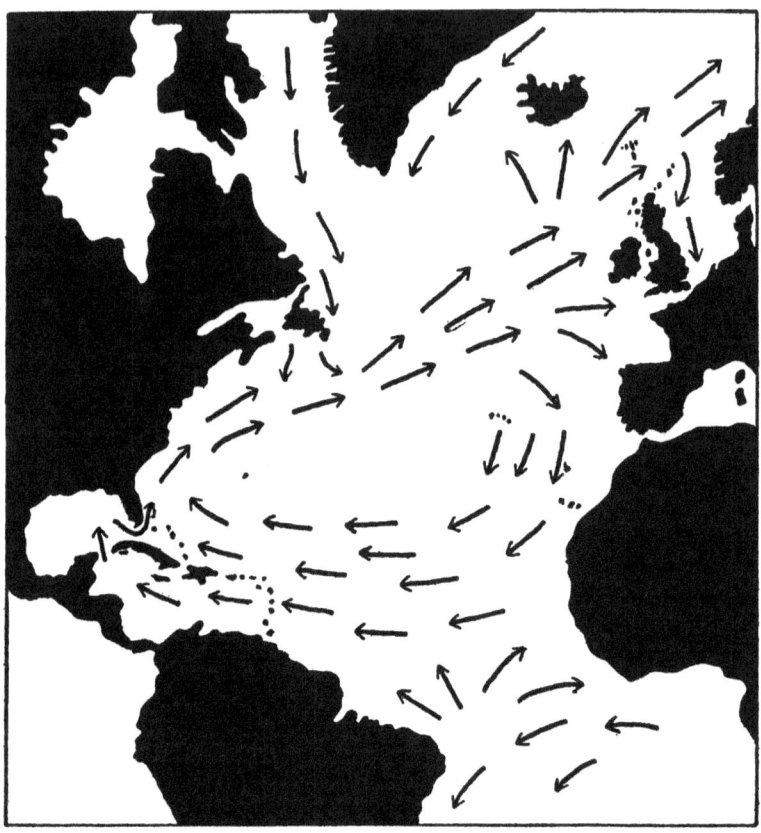

FIGURE I

The North Atlantic Ocean showing the main movements of the surface currents

In addition to the tidal streams along the shores there is a slower movement of the main waters of the sea. The movements of the surface waters of the North Atlantic Ocean are shown in Figure I. The prevailing warm easterly winds just north of the Equator blow the surface water towards the West Indies where the current turns northwards along the eastern seaboard of the United States. This warm current soon turns towards the north-

The Sea and the Shore

east, fans out and then flows slowly across the Atlantic to bathe our shores and those of Norway and of other countries in north-west Europe. This warm drift water is largely responsible for the temperate damp climate about which we are always complaining. Newfoundland and the east coast of Canada are no further north than England and yet the climate there is much colder in winter. This is because there is no warm-water current along their coast, which is washed instead by the cold Labrador current coming from the region between Arctic Canada and west Greenland. The Gulf of St. Lawrence, which is the great seaway leading to Canada's main ports, is blocked with ice in winter, whereas the English Channel ports on the same latitude, as well as many other coastlines further north in Europe, are quite free of ice at all times. The absence of ice from our coasts has greatly helped in the development of Britain into a sea-going nation.

The low spring tides are important to the naturalist because much more of the shore is then uncovered, so that animals and plants can be found and collected on the very low parts of the beach which are normally covered by water. The tides are helped by the wind, for in stormy weather the wind drives the tides a little higher up the beach than they would normally reach.

Tides and winds dominate the lives of the animals and plants of the seashore. With the rise and fall of the tides everything in the intertidal zone between high tide and low tide marks is alternately exposed to the air and submerged in sea water. The continual battering of waves on the shore, as the tide is coming in, brings many difficulties, and the exposure of the shore at low tide means that animals and plants can be dried up in hot weather or drenched with fresh water in rainy weather, or attacked by birds, rats or other animals as well as by Man. On the other hand, there are some compensations for living on the shore, for not

5

only is· there plenty of oxygen in the water available for the animals, but the light is much brighter than in deeper water, and seaweeds can grow fast.

In rocky places there are a number of ways in which animals can survive the force of the waves of incoming tides. Most of them shelter in cracks in the rocks or under seaweeds, but there are some which do not attempt to hide away but merely cling very closely to the tops and sides of the rocks: this is done by limpets and barnacles. Limpets move about in all directions when the tide is well in, but when the tide is out, or if they are being washed by the waves, each limpet will return to a sort of 'home' and cling to the rock by suction. Barnacles, on the other hand, are not able to move about like this for once they have settled down they cement themselves to the rock. Both limpets and barnacles have the same type of streamlining, so that the water flows past them easily without tearing them from the rocks.

On sandy shores the animals can gain good protection by burrowing into the sand. Some of the animals may spend their whole adult life buried in the sand, like cockles and lug-worms, while others may only retreat into the sand for short periods.

Another factor which affects the animals and plants living between tides is that in some places the saltiness (or salinity) of the sea water may differ quite a lot from the normal type of sea water from the open sea with its 35 parts of salts in 1,000 parts of sea water. Where a stream of fresh water flows down the beach the salinity of the water may be much lower. This means that many animals and seaweeds cannot live there, and that their place is taken by others which are more tolerant to fresh water. The reverse of this occurs in rock pools during very hot weather. In such conditions some of the water (but not the salts) evaporates leaving behind in the pool a relatively higher amount of salts.

The Sea and the Shore

When collecting animals and plants on the shore and when examining them afterwards it is interesting to notice how they have adapted themselves to a life between the tides, how they protect themselves from sun, rain and wind as well as from their living enemies, and how they manage to get sufficient food though uncovered during a part of each tide.

2. How the Shore was Formed

Hearken, thou craggy ocean-pyramid!
Give answer from thy voice—the sea-fowl's screams!
When were thy shoulders mantled in huge streams?
When from the sun was thy broad forehead hid?
from JOHN KEATS'S sonnet on Ailsa Craig (1818)

IT has taken many millions of years for the formation of the land and sea as we know them to-day. It is generally thought that the Earth was once a part of the sun, a burning mass of rock and metal, so hot that all was liquid and molten. A small part broke away from the sun and became the Earth. Gradually it changed as it cooled down. The outside cooled first and became a solid crust like the skin on cold porridge, but this crust was probably never even and smooth for the molten core was always pushing from the centre and forcing the crust upwards and outwards to form mountains with great hollows between them.

Time passed and water collected in the hollows between the mountain ranges, and formed the sea. But the actual shapes of the oceans and of the shorelines which form their edges have never been stable, for later movements of the Earth's crust have caused the sinking down of some parts of the dry land and the

How the Shore was Formed

emergence of new land from the sea. These have been the great movements which have formed the land and the oceans, but side by side with them, and extending over millions of years, there have been slower and less spectacular changes in the shape of the continents and seas. For as rain, frost and heat have acted on them, the softer rocks have gradually been weathered away, and the sand and dust thus formed have been washed down into the sea by streams and rivers. On the shore itself, between sea and land, the tides and waves have weathered away more rock material which has also been washed into the sea.

Over long periods of time some of the sand and mud formed in this way has collected in layers on the floor of the sea, mostly in a broad belt about 100 to 200 miles wide, round the coastlines of the world. Samples of these sand and mud deposits have been dredged up by many of the deep-sea research expeditions. As these layers have increased in number and thickness those at the bottom have been compressed and finally have become hardened to form rock. Such sedimentary rocks, formed by the gradual addition of layer to layer of sediment, can often be distinguished by the appearance of the layers or strata in which they have been deposited (Figure 2).

At different times in the history of the earth great stretches of sedimentary rocks have been lifted and bent by the violent movements of the molten mass beneath them. They have often been raised out of the sea to form new land, and sometimes they have come up at different angles so that the layers may now lie on edge instead of being level as they were when deposited on the sea floor. Much of the rock which make up the land mass of England and Scotland has been formed by this process of sedimentation. Limestone and chalk (as in the cliffs of Dover) are composed largely of the skeletons of long-dead marine animals which sank to the sea bottom. Shale and slate are compressed

9

How the Shore was Formed

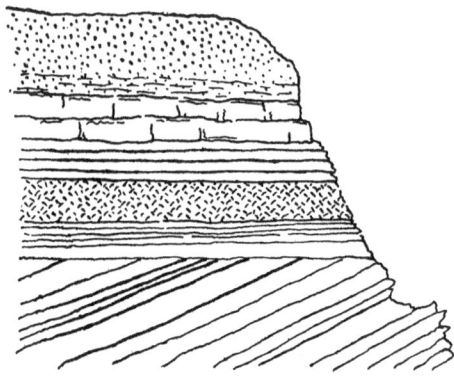

FIGURE 2

Diagram showing sedimentary strata, the layers in which many rocks
have been laid down

hardened mud, while sandstones are from deposits of sand. Coal
is also a sedimentary product, formed from the compressed
remains of plants, which grew, not in the sea, but in shallow
fresh water or even in marshland and swamp. At the present
time peat is formed in somewhat the same way in the marshy
parts of moorland.

Those rocks which are formed by the cooling of a hot molten
mass are termed igneous (from Latin, *ignis*—fire), and they include all the original rocks of the earth as well as those produced
by the more recent volcanic eruptions. Some of the cliffs along
the coasts of Britain are sedimentary, others igneous in origin.
Most of the cliffs in north-west Scotland are igneous, and so are
the granite cliffs of Land's End, the Isles of Scilly, and parts of
north Devon. On the other hand cliffs of sedimentary rock occur
more in the south and east of the country. Examples are the
chalk cliffs along the coast of Sussex, Kent, the Isle of Wight and
Dorset, and especially the very fine cliffs at Flamborough Head.
There are limestone cliffs at Torquay in Devon and near Tenby

in south Wales, and sandstone cliffs on the coasts of Caithness in the north-east corner of Scotland.

Along the south coast of England the waves come in from the south-west and therefore they arrive at an angle to the coastline, and this means that loose sand and gravel, as well as being moved up the shore towards high water, will travel along the coast towards the east. Strong wooden walls or groynes running out towards the sea have been built on many beaches along the south coast in an effort to control the drift of sand and gravel along the coast. These 'sideways' movements of beach material also occur along other parts of the British coastline.

Beaches of sand, shingle and gravel may be formed over a number of years by the action of waves mostly travelling in one direction, and then be destroyed or altered in quite a short time by a succession of gales bringing in waves which are travelling in a slightly different direction. During storms the more powerful waves move much larger stones and even boulders about on the beach. You may have noticed how a beach which was nothing but clean sand one year may have been quite transformed when seen a year or two later. Stones and boulders strewn in a band along the shore at low tide may have become half embedded in the sand, where they are a nuisance and even a danger to bathers.

There is, in fact, a continuous 'give and take' between sea and land, and while land is removed by the action of the sea in one area, it may be replaced somewhere else. It has been calculated that in the Wash an area of about 45,000 acres (seventy square miles) of land has been added to this country since the time of the Romans. Land has also been reclaimed in many other areas, including parts of Morecambe Bay, Southampton Water, the Fen area of East Anglia, and the Solway Firth in southern Scotland. Even in the comparatively short period of time represented

How the Shore was Formed

by a human life there have been changes in the coastline which can be observed and recorded. East of the Wash along the north coast of Norfolk, between Hunstanton and Blakeney Point, the coastline has been considerably altered during this century by the addition of banks and dunes of sand brought in by the sea.

Sometimes changes in the nature of the coast are brought about by windblown sand. It is recorded that a great sandstorm in the year 1694 covered an area six miles long and two miles broad in the Moray Firth, between Nairn and Burghead (N.E. Scotland). In this disaster the laird's house and sixteen prosperous and fertile farms were covered by the sands and have remained so ever since. In recent years this area, known now as the Sands of Culbin, has been planted with Corsican pines, trees which can survive on poor sandy soil, and bind the sand together with their roots.

Waves breaking in shallow water gradually build up low banks of sand or mud which increase with time. If these banks are not washed away again by winter storms, grass seeds, especially those of sand couch grass will germinate and grow into tufts which will themselves trap more sand. Gradually the banks become bound together by the branching of the grass roots. Following closely on the sand couch grass comes the next colonizer, marram grass (Figure 3a). This is the common tall grass of sand dunes; it gently pricks your legs when you walk through a patch of it. As the dunes become established and increase in height more plants arrive—among them sea holly and the little yellow stonecrop—all helping to make the sand of the dune more stable. Marram grass was planted in 1953 on the new sea walls which were being built along the east coast to replace those destroyed by the sea floods of January 1953.

Sand and shingle often form very definite features in the coastal landscape. The shingle beach at Slapton in south Devon is

FIGURE 3

(a) Marram grass, a flowering head (three-quarters natural size)
(b) Eel grass, a small plant as it appears when pulled up out of
the sand (about half natural size)

about four miles long but scarcely 100 yards wide, and behind it there is a long strip of lake. There are even larger shingle beaches at Orford Ness in Suffolk, and the Chesil Beach (eighteen miles long) between Bridport and Portland. At Dawlish, opposite Exmouth, there are two banks of sand forming Dawlish Warren. The outer of these banks has been considerably altered during the last quarter of a century.

Where the coast is low-lying quite extensive areas of land may be flooded by the sea at each high spring tide. The soil in these flooded areas, known as saltmarshes, is permanently wet, contains a lot of salt, and consists of mud which has been deposited by the incoming tides. The mud settles slowly, and here again the presence of plants helps, for the mud collects more quickly round their roots. There are saltmarshes on many parts of the coast, especially in or near river estuaries, for instance around the mouth of the Thames, along the lower reaches of the Tamar between Devon and Cornwall, and also in Cardigan Bay in Wales. Some of the best examples of saltmarsh country are along the northern coast of Norfolk, where the marshlands lie behind a string of sand dunes and shingle beaches.

New sand dunes and muddy saltmarshes may give us new areas of land in some parts of the country, but there are just as many cases of land being flooded or eaten away by the sea. Occasionally these attacks by the sea are sudden and un-expected like the tragic flooding in eastern England and in Holland at the end of January 1953. This was caused by the com-bination of an exceptionally high spring tide with strong easterly winds, which literally piled the tidal waters up the beaches and over the sea walls.

There is also a gradual erosion, or wearing away, going on around many parts of the coast. Erosion of cliffs depends very largely on the kind of rock of which they are formed. On the eastern coasts of Norfolk and Suffolk the cliffs are hard rock above with softer rock below. The sea wears away the softer rock and undermines the upper layers which eventually collapse and fall on to the beach. Erosion is also particularly heavy along the cliff coast of Yorkshire, where the rock is soft. Much of the material worn away in this area is carried southwards and deposited near Spurn Head at the mouth of the River Humber, where the shape of the coastline has changed greatly since the time of the Romans. These changes have involved both additions and losses of land, and in the course of time about twenty Yorkshire towns and villages have disappeared under the sea. Additions to the coast in Sussex have brought the town of Rye well inland, although some hundreds of years ago it was an important seaport.

As the earth became older and long after its crust had cooled down, living things in the form of simple animals and plants appeared in the sea. As these creatures died their bodies sank to the bottom and were covered by the sand and mud which collected on the sea bed. Eventually as these sediments of sand and mud increased in depth the lower ones became hardened into rock and the animal and plant remains embedded in them also became hard and preserved as fossils. These fossil remains of long-dead animals and plants are found in rocks in many places along the coast as well as inland. You will find fossil sea urchins and sea snails in the chalk rocks of south-east England, but I think the best fossil area near the sea is on the south Dorset coast. Between Lyme Regis and Charmouth the interesting ammonites and belemnites are very common in soft cliff rocks; they are the fossil skeletons of certain kinds of cuttlefishes and they occur there in great numbers.

The rocks along the coast of Yorkshire are also very rich in fossils of nearly all animal groups: this is especially true of the stretch of coast between the mouth of the River Tees and Flamborough Head. There you can find fossil ferns, sponges,

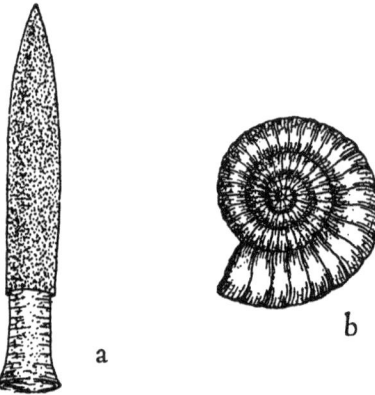

FIGURE 4

(*a*) Belemnite, and (*b*) Ammonite, the fossil remains of marine molluscs related to the common cuttle-fish

ammonites and belemnites (Figure 4) as well as the more usual mollusc and crustacean remains. There are fossil fishes in the magnesian limestone along the coast of Durham, and farther south, off Hartlepool, there is a bed of peat below the sea, with fossilized tree stumps. Peat consist of the hard compressed remains of plants and is normally formed in the marshy parts of moorland, so that this area off Hartlepool must at one time have been land which subsequently became submerged in the sea.

One of the best-known areas for fossils is in Caithness, where extensive beds of sandstone have given many interesting fossil fishes. These rocks were first worked by the Scotsman, Hugh Miller, who began life as a quarryman. Miller soon became so interested in the fossil fish which he saw in the course of his daily work that he stopped quarrying and turned all his attentions to the collection and description of the fishes and other fossils of the sandstone.

3. Seaweeds and Flowering Plants of Shore and Coast

As one who hangs down-bending from the side
Of a slow-moving boat, upon the breast
Of a still water, solacing himself
With such discoveries as his eye can make
Beneath him in the bottom of the deep,
Sees many beauteous sights—weeds, fishes, flowers,
Grots, pebbles, roots of trees, and fancies more.
WORDSWORTH in 'The Prelude'

BETWEEN tides the place of the flowering plants is taken by the seaweeds, which have no flowers, no real leaves, and no true roots. Water and the salts which are necessary for the growth of the seaweeds are absorbed from the surrounding sea water by the fronds of the weeds, and not by their holdfasts (Figure 5) which merely fix the plants to rocks and stones. Most seaweeds are flexible, and they produce from their fronds a slime (or mucus) which makes them slippery, and which prevents them from drying up when exposed to the sun's rays at low tide. Some of the seaweeds living on the shore are green in colour, while others are brown or red. The green seaweeds grow near high water mark, while the brown or olive-brown seaweeds are abundant on the main part of the shore, extending down to low water mark and below. The red weeds are not so conspicuous on the shore, where they mostly grow near low water, but they extend into deeper water than the other seaweeds, and are among the most beautiful of all shore plants.

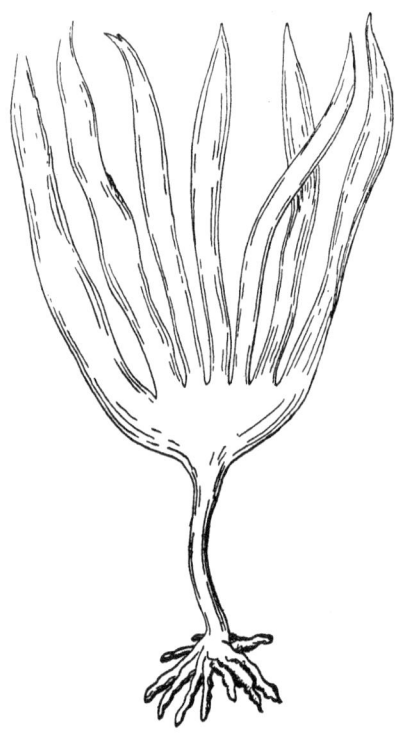

FIGURE 5

Tangle-weed (or oar-weed), showing the holdfast at the base (one-tenth natural size)

The most common of the green seaweeds is *Enteromorpha* (Figure 6)—like many others it has no English name. It grows near high water, on stones and even on mud banks, and especially where there is a trickle of fresh water flowing down the beach. Its delicate, tubular bright green fronds are often filled with small air bubbles, and in hot weather it becomes dry and white in colour. Also near high water there are usually plants of the sea lettuce with filmy green fronds, which are much eaten

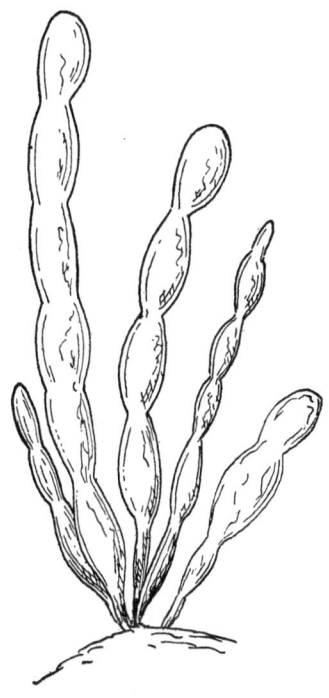

FIGURE 6

A green seaweed, *Enteromorpha*, as it appears when expanded under water. When the tide is out it lies flat and rather folded on the rocks (half natural size)

by the Japanese. The dark green hairy tufts of *Cladophora* weed are also common on the shore, especially in rock pools.

The characteristic seaweeds of the sea shore are, however, the brown wracks and tangles which grow on rocks. There is a very distinct zoning of these brown seaweeds on the shore (Figure 7), those growing at high tide being adapted to survive long exposure to the air and sun. On the other hand the brown weeds which grow near low-water mark are only exposed to the air for a few minutes twice a day. Up at high water there is a band of the channelled wrack which is often left dry for days during

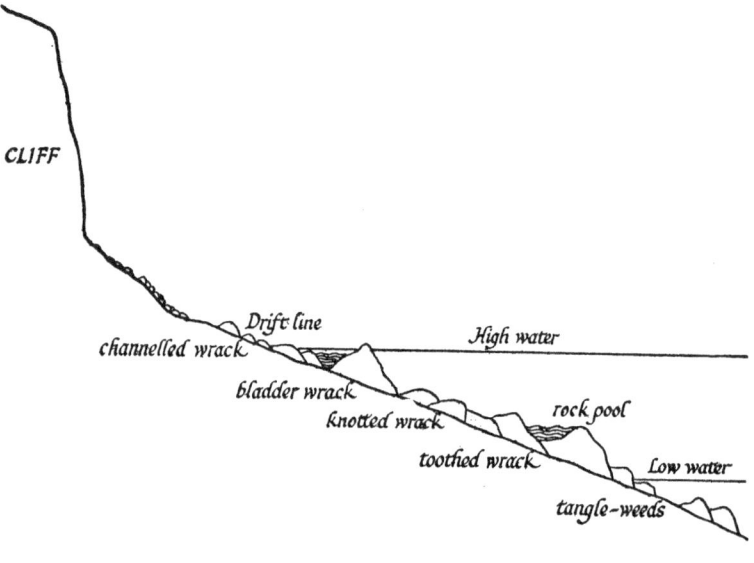

CLIFF

Drift line

channelled wrack

High water

bladder wrack

knotted wrack

rock pool

toothed wrack

Low water

tangle-weeds

FIGURE 7

A section through a typical rocky shore, from the cliffs above high tide to the waters just below low tide; also showing the zonation of the brown seaweeds

neap tides when the water does not always reach it. This is a small brown seaweed with the fronds grooved on one side. Just below it on the shore there is usually, but not always, a band of the flat wrack, a larger seaweed with smooth flattened fronds 5 to 6 inches long.

The next zone is made up of plants of the bladder wrack (Figure 8). This is the well-known seaweed with air bladders in pairs along the fronds. The air bladders help to keep the fronds afloat when the tide is in, and thus they are brought nearer to

20

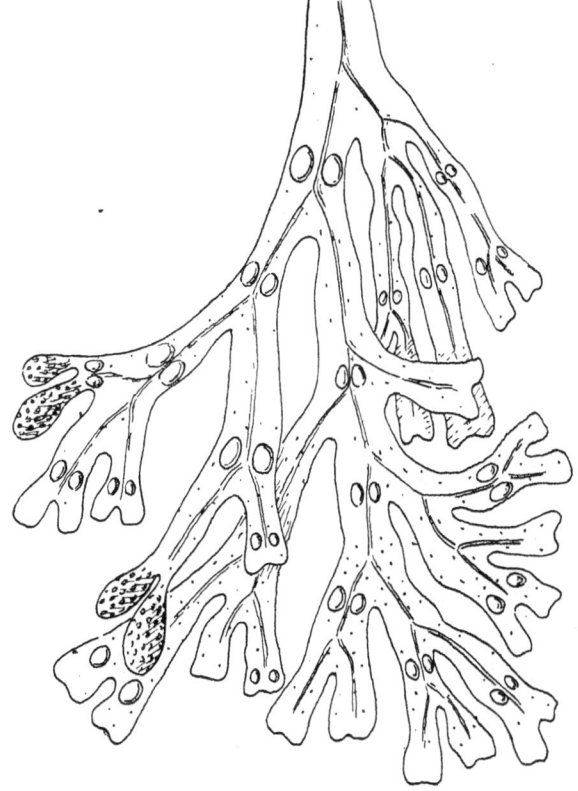

FIGURE 8

Bladder wrack (one-third natural size)

the light which is so necessary for all plant growth. Below the bladder wrack zone, around the mid-tide level, there is a wide band of the knotted wrack (Figure 9) which has long leathery fronds with larger air bladders. Below this again comes the toothed wrack (Figure 10) which extends to about low water; this seaweed has flat brown fronds with toothed edges, and usually occupies the greatest area of shore when the tide is out.

At low water and below, the wracks give place to the large

FIGURE 9

Knotted wrack (one-third
natural size)

FIGURE 10

Toothed wrack (one-third
natural size)

brown tangle-weeds, of which there are four species along the
shores of Britain. Three of these species have the main part of
the frond cut into a number of finger-like processes (Figure 5)

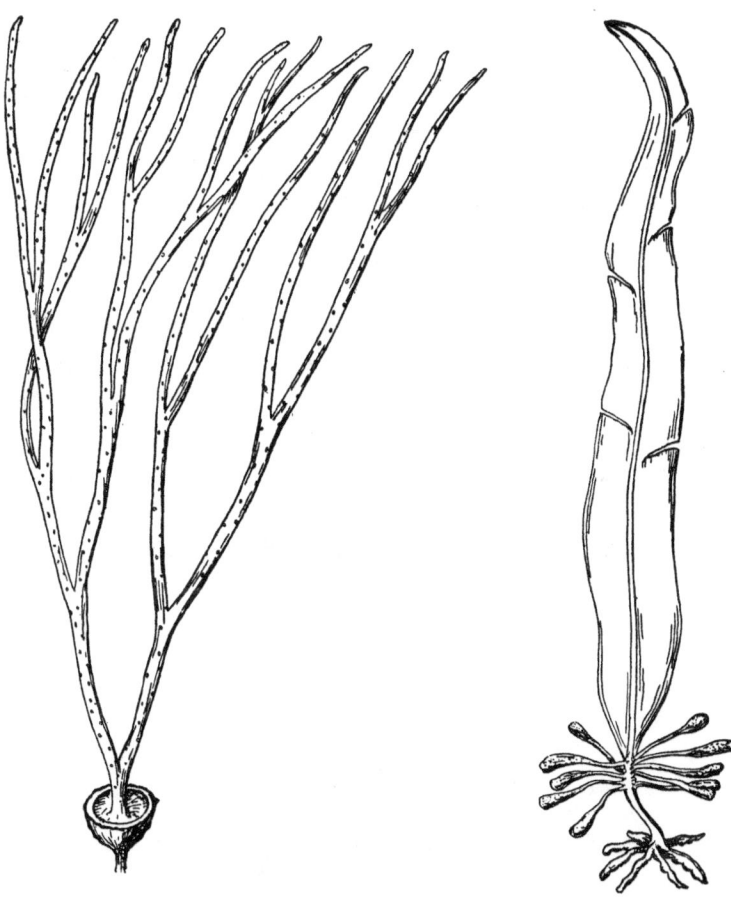

FIGURE II

Thong-weed (one-tenth natural size)

FIGURE 12

Dabberlocks, an edible
brown seaweed (one-
tenth natural size)

23

and the other species has a single long brown frond, attractively crimped at the edge and joined to the holdfast by a short stalk. The tangle weeds are really only exposed at low spring tides, when the broad flat fronds stick up out of the water and glisten in the sunlight.

Among the other brown seaweeds is the thong weed (Figure 11) which has long smooth leathery thongs which grow out from a base which looks rather like a small toadstool. In the bootlace weed the frond is like a piece of smooth slippery cord, many feet in length. It is often found washed up on sandy bathing beaches, where it trips you up when you are bathing. There is another brown seaweed, known in Scotland as dabber-locks (Figure 12) which at first looks like a tangle-weed, but it differs in having a distinct midrib to the frond. Dabberlocks is commonest in Scotland and Ireland and is not often seen in the south of England.

The red seaweeds are beautiful delicate plants, most of which grow down near low tide or below. In fact some of these weeds grow in quite deep water offshore. In rock pools and on stones

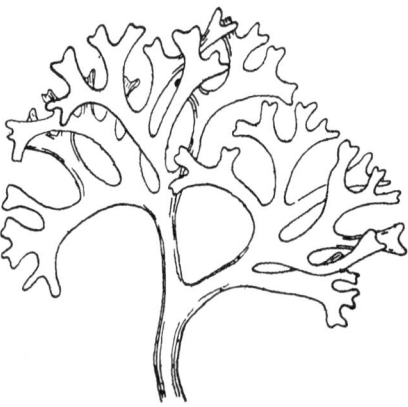

FIGURE 13

Carragheen, an edible red seaweed (three-quarters natural size)

Seaweeds and Flowering Plants of Shore and Coast

near low water you will find tufts of carragheen or Irish moss (Figure 13) and dulse (Figure 14). Very similar to carragheen

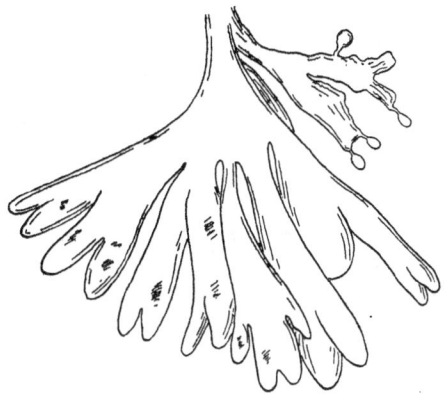

FIGURE 14

Dulse, another edible red seaweed (one-half natural size)

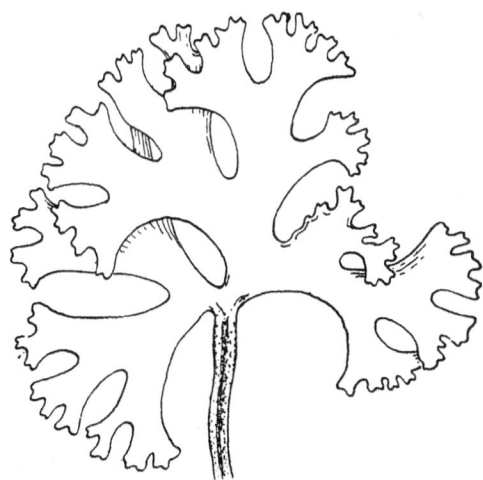

FIGURE 15

Gigartina weed, another red seaweed, very like carragheen, and probably often collected with it (three-quarters natural size)

is Gigartina weed (Figure 15), in fact they were probably collected and used together, but they can be identified by the form of the stem. In carragheen the stem is rounded or oval in cross section, while in Gigartina it has a channel running down one side. Another red seaweed known as laver, has delicate filmy fronds similar in shape to the sea lettuce, but purple-red in colour. It usually grows up near the bladder wrack zone.

There are other red seaweeds in rock pools, and two of these are very characteristic of this type of habitat. *Corallina* (coral like) is a small branching red seaweed, but instead of being soft and delicate like carragheen and dulse the fronds are covered with a hard limy coating, so that at first it is difficult even to realize that it is a plant. When the weed dies the red colour fades and the remains go pure white like chalk. *Corallina* weed forms miniature forests on the sides of rock pools and provides cover for many small animals.

Rock pools of this type often have a thick limy crust, reddish in colour. This too is a red seaweed, known as *Lithophyllum* ('stony leaf') but unlike the other seaweeds it has no stem or branching fronds.

Seaweeds have been used by Man in many parts of the world, both as a food and for other purposes. Up to about a hundred years ago considerable quantities of carragheen, dulse and laver were eaten in Scotland, Ireland, Iceland and parts of England, and even to-day one may find these weeds eaten in a few places. One way of preparing carragheen or dulse is to wash it in water for two hours, then boil it, drain off the water and mix the sea-weed pulp with oatmeal. This mixture is then pressed into cakes and fried. Among the brown seaweeds, the midrib of dabber-locks is also eaten, but on the whole seaweeds are no longer a really important source of food in Europe. It is in the Far East, and particularly in Japan, that they are still eaten in large quantities.

Along many parts of the coast farmers and market gardeners collect the driftweed washed up near high water mark and spread it on their land as a natural manure and mulch. It is especially valuable to growers of early potatoes.

Owen, writing in the sixteenth century on the subject of driftweed in south Wales said: 'After spring tides or great rigs of the sea, they fetch it in sacks on horse backes, and carie the same three, four, or five miles, and cast on the lande, which doth very much better the ground for corn and grass.'

In some places along the south coast of England the decaying drift seaweed becomes a serious nuisance where its smell drives holidaymakers from the beaches in summer. During the winter of 1953–4 there was a plague of small kelp flies in some south coast seaside towns. These flies breed in the warm, decaying driftweed. Attempts were being made to kill them by spraying, but this may have little effect on them as the flies can retreat to a depth of many inches in the sand and gravel and can stay there until the sprayed poison has washed away. It would be much better to collect the weed and put it on the land, where it would do good, instead of allowing it to rot away on the shore.

Seaweed cut fresh from the rocks can be used as a food for cattle and sheep, or in some places the animals may be allowed to browse on the shore. This is done in Scotland, where the sheep are encouraged to feed on the shore at certain times of the year. Mixed cattle foods and poultry mashes are often made up with certain content of seaweed. In Iceland dulse and dabberlocks were fed to cows during the winter when they spent most of the time in cowsheds.

In addition to these local uses of seaweed as food and manure, seaweed has had and still has many industrial uses. Records

Seaweeds and Flowering Plants of Shore and Coast

show that about 1820 one million tons of seaweed were collected every year in the Outer Hebrides and Orkney Islands and burnt in heaps on the shore to provide an ash from which soda and potash were extracted for use in making soap and glass. Then cheaper sources of soda and potash were found and this industry died out. Later in the nineteenth century there was a new demand for seaweed ash for the extraction of iodine. This too lasted for a time until new and more convenient sources of iodine were found, so that once more there was no large scale demand for seaweed.

At the present time seaweed is again in the news, for a number of other valuable substances can be made from it. Perhaps the most useful of these are the alginates which are extracted from the common brown seaweeds—the wracks and tangles. Alginates are used in ice cream to give smoothness and in processed cheese to give good spreading properties. They give a good set to jellies, certain blancmange powders and turkish delight, and are also used in emulsion paints, toothpaste, barrier creams and shaving cream. It is possible to produce alginates in fibre form and even to weave the fibres, so perhaps we may yet see 'silk' stockings made from seaweed.

The red seaweeds also give useful products. Extracts from carragheen are used in many cosmetic preparations, such as face creams, hand lotions, and sunburn lotions. Agar-agar, which is a purified jelly produced in Japan from certain red seaweeds, is of great importance in medical research work as a base on which to grow bacteria and other germs which cause disease. During the 1939-45 war the supply of agar jelly from Japan was cut off, and there was a prospect of a serious shortage of the jelly in the countries of western Europe. Fortunately, it was found that an excellent substitute, very similar to Japanese agar, could be made from carragheen and Gigartina weed.

28

Seaweeds and Flowering Plants of Shore and Coast

With our present rather limited demand for seaweed products there is not much danger of a shortage of the raw material. A recent survey of the shore zone in Scotland suggested that over much of the rocky coastline there were about 100 tons of wrack per acre. As in the last century the greatest concentration of seaweed is on the shores of the Orkney Islands and the Hebrides. Much of the coastline of Scotland below low tide has been surveyed from the air, for in aerial photographs it is possible to distinguish between rocks which are bare and those which are covered with a growth of seaweed. This air survey has shown that on the coast of Scotland there are about ten million tons of tangle-weed growing between low water mark and a depth of ten fathoms.

The flowering plants of the seashore form a fairly distinct zone around the coast, bounded on the seaward side by high water mark. Below this flowering plants are not usually found, with the exception of eelgrass, which has long, thin, tape-like green leaves and tiny inconspicuous flowers (Figure 3b), the whole plant being firmly rooted in the sand. There used to be very extensive beds of this plant in sheltered places around all our coasts, mostly at and just below low tide, and it provided a good winter food for wild geese. About 1931 the eelgrass beds started to decrease in size, both here and in other European countries, and we are now left with very little of it on our coasts. The reasons for the disappearance of the eelgrass are still not at all clear.

Above high water-mark the plant life depends largely on the amount of exposure to wind and on whether the roots of the plants are growing in sand, shingle or in pockets of soil among the rocks. Trees are never common close to the sea, because few of them can stand the force of the wind in winter. If they do grow near the sea they are usually stunted with the branches blown towards the land. It is only in very sheltered inlets of the sea, such as Salcombe in south Devon, and the Helford River in Cornwall, that you find trees with normal growth down near the water's edge. If you walk along the exposed cliffs of Cornwall all the trees are small and windswept.

It may sound strange but seaside plants suffer from a form of water shortage, even where they are being continually wetted with sea spray. The reason is that salty water is not suitable for the needs of flowering plants, because they are not able to take in the water without also taking in far too much of the salt. You therefore find that most seaside plants make do with very little water. They manage this, either by cutting down the size of their leaves so that less water evaporates from them, or by having succulent fleshy leaves which can store water. Plants by the sea are really living in desert conditions, and rationing their water supply, so that they can avoid taking up too much salt into their tissues.

On sand dunes and sandy areas in general the most important plant is marram grass, which is one of the first plants to colonize a new piece of sand bank. This grass is now specially planted in some areas, and particularly along the east coast of England, so that its roots can bind together the loose sand. In among the marram grass on sand dunes you will find sea rocket, sea campion (Figure 16), sea bindweed, sea kale (Figure 17) and in some places wild asparagus. Sea bindweed is not a climber like the bindweed of gardens and hedgerows, but sends out long trailing stems across the sand.

On sea cliffs and rocky ledges, thrift, samphire and scurvy grass are common. Thrift is the plant shown up to 1952 on the reverse of the twelve-sided threepenny piece, but now, unfortunately replaced by another design. Scurvy grass (Figure 18) is common on muddy shores as well as on rocks, and its white flowers are out from May to August. The leaves were at one

FIGURE 16

Sea campion (three-quarters natural size)

time eaten to prevent scurvy; they are fleshy and their sharpness makes a good addition to a green salad. The leaves of samphire also have a pleasant sharp taste, and I have found them excellent as an addition to home-made pickles.

Wild beet is found on muddy shores, but I have seen it more commonly at the foot of cliffs in Cornwall. It is a large handsome plant, the ancestor of our garden and sugar beet. At the top of the cliffs you occasionally find wild cabbage and asparagus, usually in sandy soil, but they are rare and the cabbage is only likely to be found in the south of England. The succulent

31

FIGURE 17
Sea kale (one-half natural size)

Lower leaves like this

FIGURE 18

Scurvy grass (three-quarters natural size)

tasty asparagus grown in gardens was developed from the wild asparagus, and it is one of the few garden plants which do not mind a sprinkling of salt.

Shingle beaches are interesting, although they are not common in Britain. On the shingle at Slapton, in south Devon, I have found that in August the main flowering plants are Sea Purslane, Blue Gromwell, Yellow Horned Poppy (Figure 19), Sea Spurge, and Sea Campion (Figure 16). Of these the most impressive is the Yellow Horned Poppy, which has beautiful clear yellow flowers and grey-green leaves. As the yellow petals fall the remainder of the flower ripens into the long curved

D

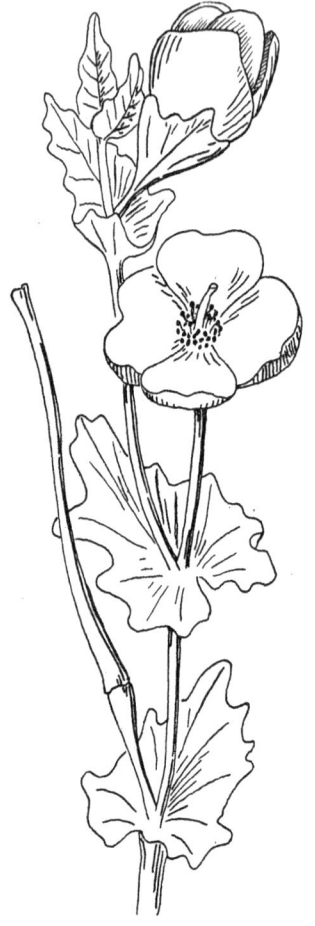

FIGURE 19

Yellow horned poppy (one-half natural size)

'horn' which contains the seeds.

In saltmarshes protected from the sea by a dune or seawall, the soil is usually flooded by the sea at irregular intervals, and it is permanently salty and damp. Sea plantain, glasswort, seablite and many grasses and rushes are common in these places, as well as the sea aster which looks like an untidy Michaelmas daisy; its flowers have a yellow central disc and bluish-purple outer rays, and the leaves are small and fleshy. Sea lavender is also a salt-marsh plant—this is a kind of 'everlasting flower', such as are sold in flower shops in winter, and is nothing like the common scented garden lavender.

The land at the top of many cliffs is often covered by a soft mat of grass, kept short and fine by the regular browsing of rabbits. There you may see violets and thyme and many other plants more commonly found inland, but in addition you can often find the autumn squill, a miniature hyacinth with starry blue flowers and long thin leaves growing out from a small bulb. I last found this attractive plant growing on sandy ground at the top of cliffs in the Channel Islands, where it was flowering in September.

These and many other plants will give added interest to a walk along the cliffs and beaches, and if you are attracted by a plant try not to dig up great masses of it in the hope of getting it to grow in the garden at home. Certainly many seaside plants will grow in the garden, and if you want to try take only a small root or a couple of bulbs. Then you will not be damaging a piece of cliff pasture which is the result of many years growth.

It is interesting to notice the large number of seaside plants which have been selected and developed to give us our common kitchen-garden vegetables. Wild cabbage, sea kale, carrot, beet, asparagus are all seashore or sea cliff plants of which the best forms have been taken into cultivation. These plants all have fleshy leaves, which makes them good eating when cooked. Sea blite is also edible, and the taste is almost the same as that of spinach, to which it is related, but it takes a long time to get the small leaves off the tough wiry stems, so I cannot advise you to try it except as an interesting experiment.

4. Fishes of the Seashore

You see the way the Fisherman doth take
To catch the Fish; what Engins doth he make?
Behold how he ingageth all his wits,
Also his Snares, Lines, Angles, Hooks, and Nets.
Yet fish there be, that neither Hook, nor Line,
Nor Snare, nor Net, nor Engin can make thine;
They must be gropt for, and be tickled too,
Or they will not be catch't, whate'er you do.
                    From JOHN BUNYAN's *Pilgrim's Progress*

ALONG all the coasts of Britain, in rock pools and in sandy places at low tide, you will find fishes lurking and waiting for the return of the tide. Although there are quite a number of different species of shore fishes, most of them can be identified quite easily, and they are not difficult to catch.

Fishes and birds, like man, rabbits, whales, frogs and snakes, all have a backbone made up of a number of joints or vertebrae, and they are known as vertebrate animals, to distinguish them from the invertebrates, animals which have no backbones, such as crabs, prawns, sea anemones, starfishes, ragworms and many others. The backbone of the vertebrates acts as a main support for the whole body and also as a base for the attachment of the paired limbs. The jointing of the backbone and limbs allows a

36

great amount of movements, and some vertebrates are among the fastest moving of all living things. In fishes both pairs of limbs form fins, in birds the front limbs are developed into wings for flying and the same has happened in the bats. In other vertebrates, such as frogs, toads, lizards and in the warm-blooded mammals (rats, rabbits, whales, dogs, cats, seals, moles, hedgehogs and many more) both pairs of limbs are used for walking, running, jumping or digging. In snakes and slow-worms the limbs are lost or so much reduced that there is no sign of them from the outside. In Man the front limbs are de-veloped into arms with hands which can acquire great skill in making things.

In fishes the paired limbs are known as the pectoral (or breast) fins and pelvic fins. In the herring (Figure 21) the pectoral fins

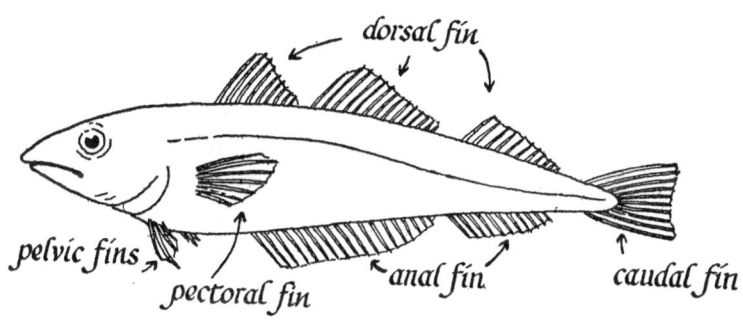

FIGURE 20

Whiting, outline diagram to show fin arrangement

are just behind the head and the pelvic fins are further back to-wards the tail, but in many fishes, and certainly in most of the shore fishes, the pelvic fins have moved forward to a position near the pectoral fins; this can be seen in the whiting (Figure 20). In addition to the paired fins fishes have unpaired fins along the back (dorsal fins), on the belly (anal fin) and round the tail

Fishes of the Seashore

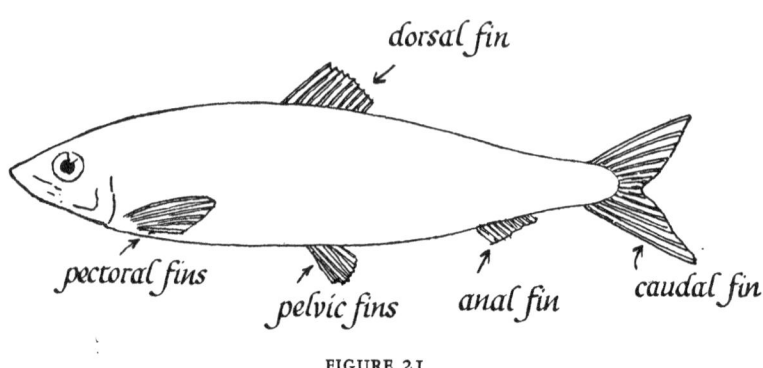

FIGURE 21

Herring, outline diagram to show fin arrangement

(caudal fin). These fins vary in position and extent in different fishes, and are useful in distinguishing the species.

Fishes are among the most important animals in the sea and they form a great supply of food for Man. Most of the large fisheries of the world are based on areas where a few species of fish are especially abundant, and usually within 100 miles of land. In the North Atlantic there are cod fisheries on the Great Banks of Newfoundland, in the waters off West Greenland, Iceland and Scotland, and herring fisheries round Iceland, Orkney and Shetland, and along the east coast of England and Scotland. In the south-west of England there is a mackerel fishery, and in some months a pilchard fishery along the south coast of Cornwall.

Flatfish, such as plaice and dab, begin life as small fishes looking like very tiny cod or whiting but they later settle on the bottom and lie on one side. The eye which is then on the underside moves over to the top side and comes to lie near the other eye, and the whole body becomes more and more flattened from side to side. There are also other flat fishes, the rays and skates (Figure 22) which are flattened from back to belly, and not from

38

side to side. They swim by a wavy motion of the outer edges of the body, known to fishermen as the 'wings'.

Bony fishes often drink water, and you will sometimes see them open their mouths as though they were drinking. When

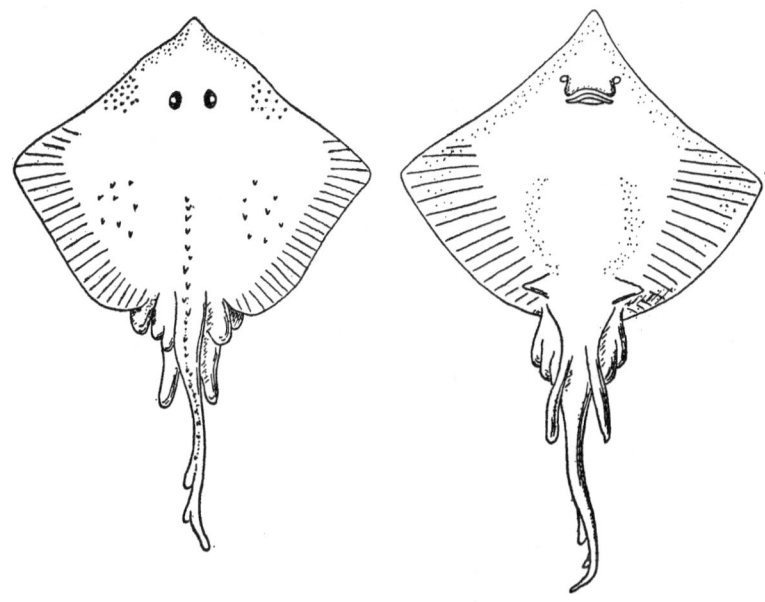

FIGURE 22

(*a*) Thornback ray, upper surface (one-tenth natural size)
(*b*) Skate, lower surface (one-tenth natural size)

they do this the water is usually being passed from the mouth, over the gills and out through the gill slits; by this means the air dissolved in the water is able to aerate and freshen the blood which comes close to the surface in the gills.

Most shore fishes are dark or mottled in colour, and they blend very closely with the background against which they are living. Some are able to change their colour if the background colour is changed. This happens in the gobies and in the offshore flat-

39

fishes such as plaice and brill, but you will find that the rocklings cannot do this and they always remain dark, almost black, even when placed in a white dish.

Shore fishes are adapted to a life of hiding away in rock pools and under large stones; some of them even hide in the sand. They are not strong swimmers like herring and mackerel, and they usually move in quick short bursts of speed. On the whole shore fishes are not difficult to distinguish as they nearly all have some peculiarity in shape which will make their identity quite obvious if they are compared with the sketches.

Like all animals they are classified into groups according to the shape and form of the body and internal organs. The following list will give some idea of the main groups of fishes found in the seas around Britain. The names in brackets are sea fishes which are not normally found between tidemarks or even just below low tide.

I. *Fishes with cartilage (gristle) instead of bone*
   (Dogfish, shark, ray, skate)
II. *Fishes with true bones*
   (*a*) (Herring, pilchard and sprat family)
   (*b*) (Salmon and trout family)
   (*c*) Eels
   (*d*) Sticklebacks
   (*e*) Pipe-fishes
   (*f*) Sand eels
   (*g*) Grey mullet
   (*h*) Cod family. Rockling on the shore. (Cod, whiting, and
      haddock in deeper water)
   (*i*) Blennies and butterfish
   (*j*) Weever fish
   (*k*) Sucker fish
   (*l*) Gobies

Fishes of the Seashore

(*m*) Flatfish; plaice, dab, flounders, sole

(*n*) Wrasse

(*o*) Gurnards, bullheads, pogge and lumpsuckers

(*p*) Bass

(*q*) (Mackerel)

Many of these fishes can be found on rocky or sandy shores, but in most cases they need to be looked for, as they lie as hidden as possible when the tide is out.

The conger eel is common on rocky coasts. It may grow to a length of five feet, but only the smaller ones are found near the shore. It is one of the few fishes in which the back, tail and anal fins are all continuous. The body is almost the same thickness along its whole length, and is covered with steel-grey skin, with no obvious scales. Congers have a large mouth armed with teeth and will snap at anything within reach, and more particularly at moving objects. They are not uncommonly seen in the waters just below low water, but they should be avoided as a conger bite could give a bad wound. In north Wales they are caught in rocky places by means of a long instrument looking like a shepherd's crook.

In fresh water there are two kinds of stickleback, the three-spined, which is very common, and the ten-spined. In the sea we have the fifteen-spined stickleback (Figure 23), a slender fish about five inches long, with fifteen spines along the back, and a

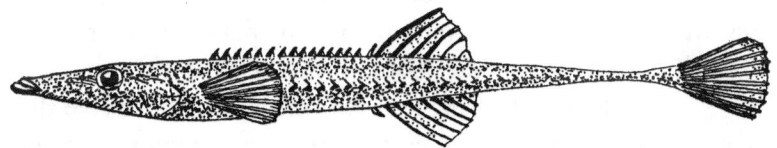

FIGURE 23

Sea stickleback (= 15-spined stickleback). (Two-thirds natural size)

long snout ending in a small mouth. Most of the body is

Fishes of the Seashore

greenish-brown with silvery white on the belly and under the head. They live in rocky places near the shore, especially among thick seaweed, where they feed on small, almost microscopic animals.

In the spring at the start of the breeding season the male sticklebacks become much more highly coloured than the females, and they build a nest out of pieces of seaweed. The nest is usually built in the bottom, stiffer branches of wracks and tangle-weeds, and it may remind you of the nest of a reed warbler or harvest mouse. When the nest is finished the male fish chases the female into it and she then lays her eggs in the middle. More than one female may lay eggs in each nest. After the eggs have been laid the females go away, but the male remains and very attentively guards the nest until the young sticklebacks hatch out. At this time the males are very ferocious and will attack other male sticklebacks or even other fish which come near. The nests are usually built below low water mark, but I have sometimes found adults in pools further up the shore.

Sea sticklebacks are attractive creatures to keep in a small aquarium, as they spend a lot of time swimming about and do not hide away behind rocks. For feeding you will need some tiny 'plankton' animals, each one rather smaller than a pin head. If your aquarium is inland and you cannot get such a food supply then try the water fleas of about the same size which you can collect from a freshwater pond with a small muslin net, but it is best to drain off the fresh water before you put the water fleas in with the sticklebacks. You may find that if the sticklebacks are large (about four to five inches long) they will not survive the winter. This is quite normal because, so far as we know, sticklebacks which have reared a brood of young do not usually live on into the following summer.

The long, thin pipe-fishes live hidden in weeds and especially among eelgrass at low tide. They are slow fish, and usually swim by means of the delicate quivering movement of the back fin. This method of movement is also used by the sea horses which belong to the same family of fishes. Both sea horses and pipe-fishes have small round mouths and they feed on marine water fleas and other tiny animals. In pipe-fishes it is once again the male which guards the eggs, but he does not build a nest for them. Instead he carries them around in a slit pouch which runs along the underside of his body, until they are hatched. Even when they are swimming freely the tiny young pipe-fishes will often swim back into this brood pouch if they are being chased. On the shores among weeds and eelgrass near low tide you will find two or three different pipe-fishes, all with rather angular bodies, but at mid-tide or thereabouts you should find yet another pipe-fish with a very thin, smooth, worm-like body, a tiny eye and no real tail fin. This little pipe-fish lives out of water when the tide is low, sheltering under stones. When you find it in this sort of place it looks more than ever like a worm, because its back fin is folded down close to the body, but put it in a jar of water and you will soon see that it is a fish and not a worm.

At one moment you may see a fine shoal of blue-green sand eels swimming peacefully in a sand pool, but take another pace towards them and they will have disappeared, nose first into the sand. Sand eels make an excellent bait for fishing and they are much collected by fishermen. To catch them it is no use digging as they can burrow much faster than a man can dig with a spade. Instead you will find that in most parts of the country they are hooked out of the sand. The hook used by fishermen is a piece of bent iron rod twelve to eighteen inches long. With this instrument the fisherman slashes through the sand, catching on the bodies of the sand eels, and dragging them out of the sand.

Fishes of the Seashore

Grey mullet are common in shallow waters, often in harbours, and young specimens two to three inches long may be found between tidemarks. They are dark grey-green in colour, lighter on the sides and belly, and have rather prominent lips. They are not an easy fish to catch in open water, as they are not much attracted by living food; in fact a good part of their natural food is seaweed. Grey mullet should not be confused with red mullet, a fish found in deeper water, and perhaps one of the best flavoured things in the sea. The Romans used to pay fantastic sums of money for good fresh red mullet to eat at their banquets. The writer, Suetonius, mentions that on one occasion 30,000 sesterces—about £250—were given for three mullets, and there is also a record of £48 being given for a single mullet weighing six pounds. In the larger Roman banquets, the fish were often brought to the table alive, probably in special open ducts, before they were taken away to the kitchen. By this method there could be no doubt that they were eaten fresh. I like red mullet best when it has been cooked in cider in a casserole.

The fishes of the cod family are perhaps a disappointing meal after these thoughts of red mullet. Nevertheless they are the most important of all to the fishing industry in north-west Europe. They are mainly caught by trawlers which are based in Hull, Grimsby, Fleetwood, Aberdeen, Milford Haven and many smaller ports. Most of a trawler's catch is cod, whiting, hake and haddock, all powerful free-swimming fish living in great shoals in the open sea. The pollack is a fish of the cod family which you can fish for from jetties and piers and also from rocks on the shore, using a rod and line. It is really one of the easiest fish to catch in this way. You can tell a pollack from a whiting quite easily—the pollack has its lower jaw projecting beyond the upper jaw, whereas the whiting has a longer upper jaw, also the pollack has a darker skin than the whiting.

Fishes of the Seashore

On the shore the family is represented by the rocklings, which are thick-set fishes living near the bottom between tides as well as in deeper water. In all the rocklings the first dorsal fin is very short when seen from the side; this fin flickers rather like the edge of a flag in a wind, and it is possible that it acts as a tasting organ to detect the presence of food in the water.

Rocklings are seldom seen on a casual walk along the shore, for they hide away under rocks covered with seaweeds. There are three species, all of which are dark, almost black, but they can easily be distinguished by the number of fleshy barbs which project from the jaws. In the Three-bearded Rockling which may reach a foot or more in length the lower jaw has one barb and the upper jaw has two barbs. These barbs are like that on the lower jaw of a cod; in the living fish they always project forwards and act as feelers which can sense food on the bottom as the fish swims along. Whiting and pollack, which are not bottom-feeders, do not have barbs. The Five-bearded Rockling (Figure 24) is similar in general appearance to the last species,

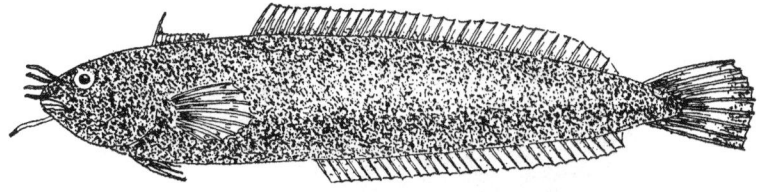

FIGURE 24

Five-bearded rockling (two-thirds natural size)

but smaller, and it has four barbs on the upper jaw and one on the lower jaw. This is the common rockling of the shore. The Four-bearded Rockling, a much rarer fish found in offshore waters has three barbs on the upper and one on the lower jaw.

The blennies are true shore fishes—bad swimmers with thick

Fishes of the Seashore

clumsy bodies, variable colouring, and a liking for hiding away
in holes. The Tompot blenny (Figure 25) is one of these fussy

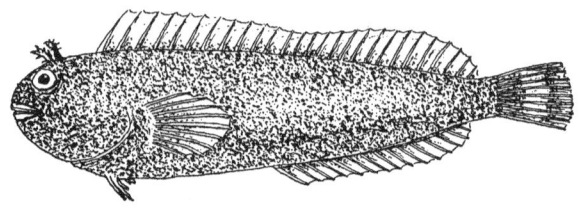

FIGURE 25
Tompot blenny (two-thirds natural size)

aggressive little fishes, which you will find in rocky places,
especially along the south coast. In the aquarium at Plymouth I
have watched a small Tompot blenny being turned out of a
submerged Bovril bottle by a larger one. Their staring eyes and
jerky movements reminded me of a circus clown. They have a
fringed crest above each eye, which distinguishes them from the
Shanny or Smooth blenny (Figure 26) which has no crests. The

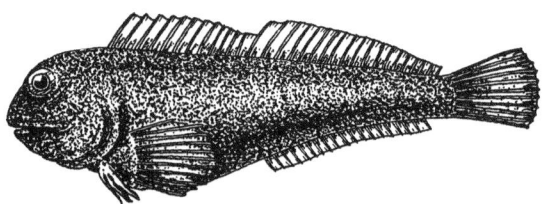

FIGURE 26
Shanny or smooth blenny (two-thirds natural size)

Shanny lives in the same sort of place as the Tompot blenny, and
it also appears to have a territory or small area which it regards
as its own, and from which it will drive off other Shanny. The
female lays her eggs in rock crevices where the male fish guards

46

them until they are hatched. Shannies are a favourite food of cormorants and shags. In the south-west of England you may come across Montagu's blenny which is smaller than the other blennies and is easily distinguished from them by having a single crest on the top of the head.

In the deeper offshore waters we often trawl up the beautiful Butterfly blenny (Figure 27). It has a crest above each eye like

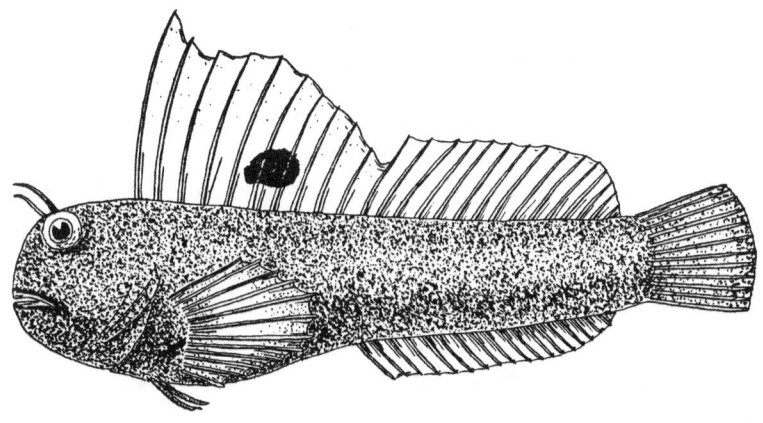

FIGURE 27

Butterfly blenny, a fish from offshore (two-thirds natural size)

the Tompot blenny from which it differs in having a much taller dorsal fin marked with a large dark blue 'eye-spot' not unlike the vivid spots on the tail feathers of a peacock.

A related fish, the Eel-pout or Viviparous blenny, is also found sometimes on the shore, but usually only along the east coast of England and Scotland. The female Eel-pout does not lay eggs, but the young pass their early stages inside her body and are born as fully formed small fish, about four months after the mating which takes place in August or September.

The Butterfish or Gunnel (Figure 28), is an attractive shiny eel-like fish, about four to six inches long, and flattened from side to side. The back fin runs the whole length of the body behind the head, and the anal fin runs forward from the tail

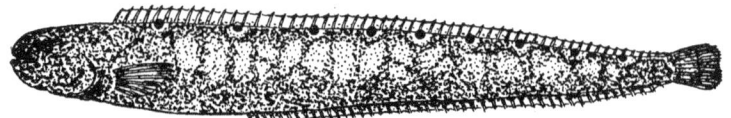

FIGURE 28

Butterfish, or gunnel (two-thirds natural size)

along the underside for about half the length of the body. There are eight to twelve round black spots at intervals along the dorsal fin, each spot circled in white or yellow, and standing out prominently when seen against the yellow-brown marbled colouring of the body. The eggs are laid in the winter (December–March), often in an empty shell, and they are guarded by both parents but more usually by the male. I have often found the eggs laid in empty scallop shells, but only once have I seen the eggs guarded by one of the parents.

The Viper Weever (Figure 29) is a small fish four to five inches long which lives in sandy places on the shore. Weevers bury themselves in the sand by the movement of the anal fin

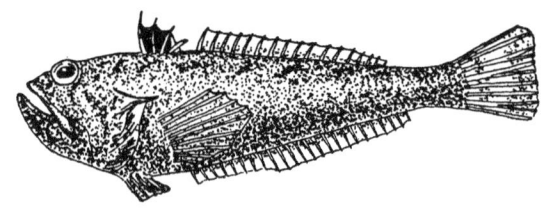

FIGURE 29

Viper weever. The first spine of the dorsal fin, and the spine on the gill flap (operculum) are poisonous (two-thirds natural size)

until only the dorsal fin is visible above the surface. They are usually yellow with brown markings except the front dorsal fin which is black: the first spine on this fin as well as the strong spine on the back edge of the gill cover are connected with poison sacs and inflict painful wounds on the bare feet of bathers. The poison can cause great pain and anyone stung by a weever should go straight to a doctor who will know how to treat the wound. The poison does not affect the nervous system but acts by attacking the red corpuscles of the blood and by stopping the white corpuscles from doing their job of keeping the blood clean. Like the conger eel this is a fish to avoid.

The Cornish Sucker (Figure 30) is a small shore fish, up to four inches, broader at the head end, and flattened from back to belly. The upper parts are dark purple with pink or red markings

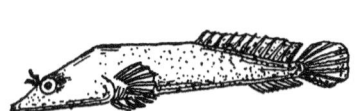 

FIGURE 30

Cornish sucker, seen from the side and from below (three-quarters natural size)

and behind each eye there is a purple spot edged with a pale yellow ring. Also on the head near the eyes there are two little crests not unlike those seen on the Tompot blenny. On the belly which is pale red there is a strong sucker by means of which the fish clings to flat rocks; it can, in fact, cling on to rocks and stones very firmly, much more firmly than the gobies which also have a sucker on the underside. The Cornish Sucker feeds on sandhoppers and other small animals. It lays its eggs under

E

stones, and will stay nearby and guard them even when the tide is out.

Like the blennies the gobies form another distinct group of shore fishes. The Rock goby (Figure 31) is one of the longer species, reaching a length of six to eight inches. The colour

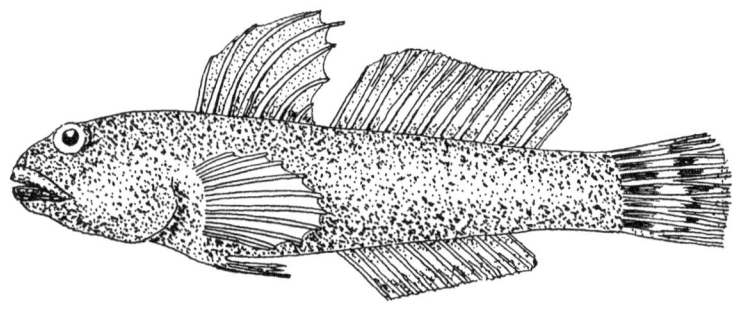

edge always pale →

1st dorsal fin of Paganelle goby

FIGURE 31

Rock goby, and dorsal fin of paganelle goby (three-quarters natural size)

varies greatly according to the shade of the ground on which the fish is living. Normally they are grey-brown mottled with dark brown and yellow when living in the shadow of rocks on the shore or just below low water mark, but if placed in a white dish they become much paler in the course of a few hours. They feed mainly on crustaceans or worms, and are able to attach themselves to rocks and stones by a sucker in the middle of the underside. This sucker is actually formed by the two pelvic fins.

The Paganelle goby is similar in shape to the Rock goby,

usually not so long, and with a more regular edge to the first dorsal fin. In the Rock goby this fin has a definite crested appearance. This difference is best seen in the drawings. The Paganelle also has a pale band along the top of the first dorsal fin (Figure 31). This band is always present, but is more obvious in spring and summer during the breeding season.

The Two-spot goby (Figure 32) is a much smaller fish, seldom more than 2½ inches long and marked with a dark spot where the tail joins the body and another spot at each side of the body just behind the pectoral fin. They live mostly just below low-water mark and they differ from the other gobies in being pelagic, that is they swim and feed in the open water well above the bottom, whereas the other species are found hidden among seaweeds and rocks.

The Sand goby is found in sandy places especially in the sand pools left when the tide is out, and which it shares with the common shrimp. Sand gobies build a nest for their eggs, usually

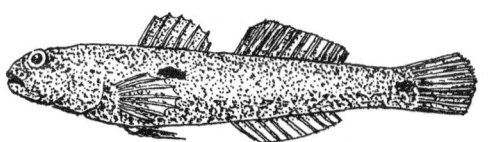

FIGURE 32

Two-spot goby (three-quarters natural size)

under an empty shell. I have seen a Sand goby which had laid its eggs under an empty queen scallop shell in a sandy-bottomed aquarium tank. One of the parent fish used to guard the eggs and when it was in position only the tip of its snout appeared below the edge of the shell.

Most flatfish live in deep water offshore, where they are valuable as a source of first-class fish; these are especially plaice, halibut, sole, brill and turbot. On the shore one occasionally finds the young of these fishes, usually when they are one to two inches long. The only adult flatfish found commonly on the shore are flounders and lemon dabs.

Flounders (or flatties) (Figure 33) sometimes remain in sand pools when the tide goes out and they are also fished in the sandy parts of river estuaries, and will even go far up some

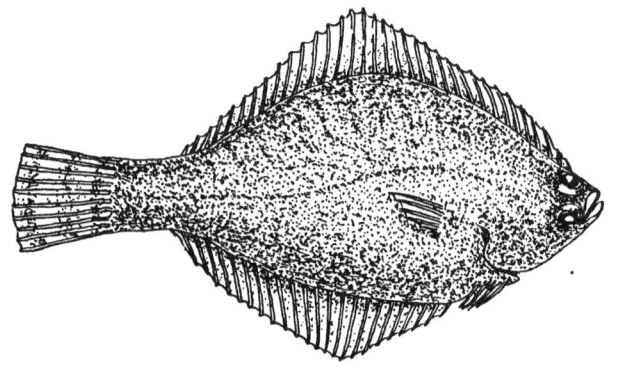

FIGURE 33

Flounder (one-quarter natural size)

rivers, into water which is quite fresh. They only have very small scales, unlike plaice which have well-developed scales, but the best way to distinguish these two fishes is to run your finger carefully along one edge of the body (near the base of the fins) from tail to head. If you meet short spines then the fish is a flounder, if this edge is smooth and without spines then you have a plaice. You can often catch flounders with a hand net if you walk carefully through the larger sand pools.

Dabs (Figure 34) are also found in sandy places and in river estuaries, where they are fished with hook and line. They may be up to twelve inches long, and are yellow-brown in colour, with darker brown mottling, and the upper side is rough all

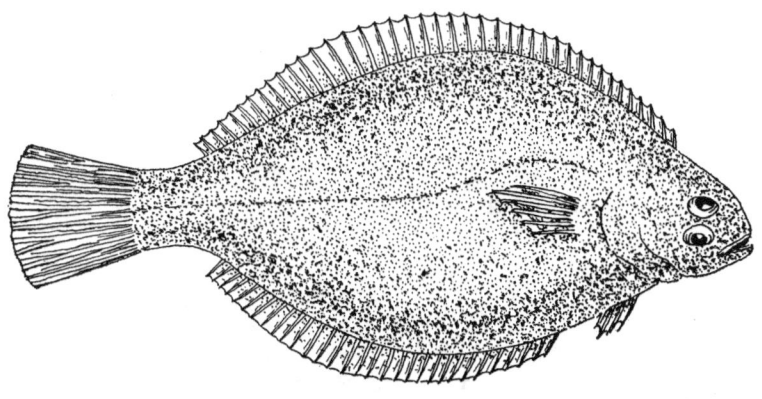

FIGURE 34
Dab (one-quarter natural size)

over when rubbed from tail to head. For more details on how to distinguish flatfishes see p. **143**

The wrasses are typical fish of the shallow, rock-strewn waters which occur along many parts of the British coast. The Latin name of the family *Labridae* (from *labrum*, a lip) refers to the very pronounced lips which occur in all species; they also have strong teeth which they use in feeding on mussels, small crabs and worms taken from the rocks among which they live. They are not easy to watch in their natural home unless you are a diver, but from observations in an aquarium there is no doubt that they have a sense of territory, for they will drive away other fish, especially other wrasse, from their favourite ledges and rocks.

The Ballan wrasse (Figure 35) is the largest species, and lives among the seaweed-covered rocks just below low-water mark. They are sometimes taken by sea anglers along the south coast and the young are caught by cormorants and shags. They have been known to reach a length of sixteen inches, and a weight of eight pounds, but a good average specimen is ten to twelve inches long. The colour is very variable, but is usually yellow-green, with red markings on the edges of the scales, so that the body appears to be covered with a pattern of large spots. The young do not show this spotted skin so well. The eggs are laid by the female in a rough nest made of seaweed and shells, and they are guarded by the male until the young hatch out.

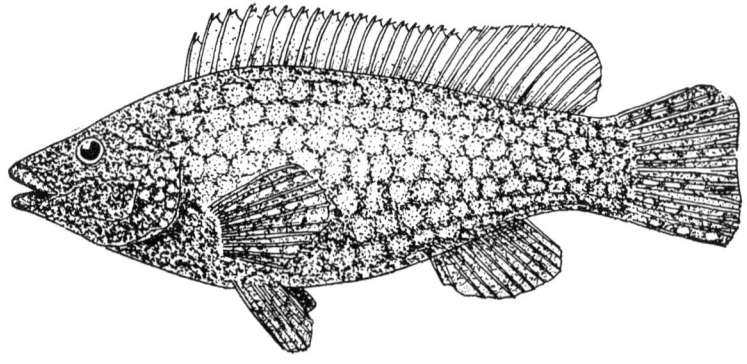

FIGURE 35
Ballan wrasse (one-third natural size)

The Corkwing wrasse or Conner is much smaller, usually five to six inches long and coloured brown on the upper parts, with green or red bands near the gill covers. There is a dark spot near the *middle* of the base of the tail (at the end of the lateral line) and this is a character of the species. They live very close to the low-water mark and are especially common in the West Country.

The Rock wrasse or Jago's goldsinny (Figure 36) is the other common wrasse, especially in the west of England and along the coasts of Scotland. It reaches about the same size as the Conner, and is distinguished from it by the position of the black spot near the tail. In the goldsinny this spot is at the upper border of the base of the tail, and there is also a dark spot at the front of the dorsal fin. On a calm day you can sit and watch goldsinny and

54

Fishes of the Seashore

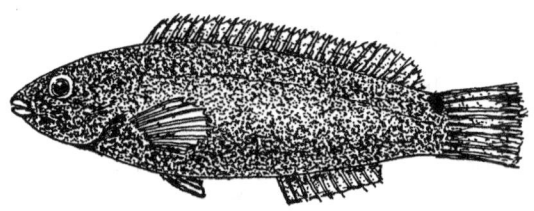

FIGURE 36
Rock wrasse (three-quarters natural size)

corkwing wrasse from the tops of steep rocks on the Cornish coast.

The Rock cook is a small-mouthed wrasse, about three to four inches long, with a dark red back, and a paler belly. Its main distinguishing character is a broad dark marking (not a single spot) between the upper margin of the tail and the back end of the dorsal fin.

The Cuckoo wrasse is the most brightly coloured of all British fishes. It would scarcely be found on the shore, but is not uncommon on rocky coasts below low-water mark. You can fish for it with a rod and line in places where the rocks drop down steeply into the sea. The interesting thing about this wrasse is that the male and female are entirely different in colour, just like the domestic cock and hen. In fact at one time they were thought to be different species. In the male the head and most of the back is yellow, shading into orange near the tail. The fins are red, but the dorsal and anal fins often have a blue border. Running along the yellow or orange colouring of the back there are bright purple or blue bands, and there are similar but shorter bands on the head. In the female Cuckoo wrasse the body colour is not nearly so bright, but is beautiful vermilion red, paler on the belly, and with three or four dark spots on the back near the dorsal fins.

Fishes of the Seashore

The colours of the Cuckoo wrasse, and especially of the male fish are among the most striking that you will see in British waters. In some lights the bright blues of the male take on a metallic sheen which gives changes of shade and tone as the fish swims lazily before you. Many people who see a male Cuckoo wrasse for the first time in an aquarium will scarcely believe that such a fish lives along the coast of Britain, for it would indeed fit perfectly into the brilliant background of a tropical coral reef.

A common fish living just below low water is the Bass, a great favourite with sea anglers, who use a bait of sand eel or a piece of herring when fishing for it. Bass have no special peculiarity of shape or colour, and I always think they are the dullest of all the shore fishes. They do, however, have spiny dorsal fins which can give bad wounds if they are handled carelessly.

The bullheads are small ugly spiny fish. One species, the Miller's Thumb is a freshwater fish, but the other two, the Father Lasher and the Sea Scorpion, are typical shore fish, clumsily built, and swimming in and out of rocks in short bursts of speed. When taken out of the water they make a low-pitched grunting noise, produced by the movement of the gill covers. Both species are spiny, and the spines are especially poisonous during the breeding season, which is from December to April. The best way to distinguish them is to finger carefully along the lateral line which runs along the side of the body. In the Father Lasher this is quite smooth but in the Sea Scorpion it has a row of small bony scales which are rough to the touch. Both fish feed on any small animals, usually young fish and crabs, in fact they should never be put into aquarium tanks with small fish, such as wrasse or blennies or they will eat them up in a very short time.

Fishes of the Seashore

The Pogge (Figure 37) is another shallow-water fish, about four to five inches long, with an attractive and characteristic turned-up snout and hard spines on the head and gill covers. It is quite common along the south coast but perhaps commoner

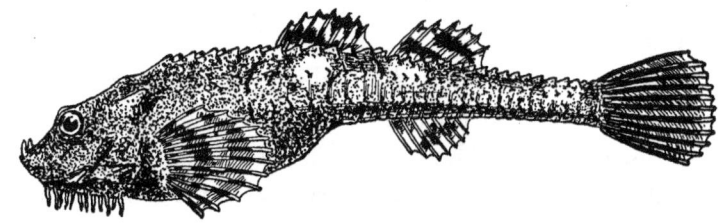

FIGURE 37

Pogge (three-quarters natural size)

along the shores of the North Sea. I have found them when the tide was out in the little rock pools formed at the base of boulders.

The lumpsucker is a stout thickset fish with a sucker on the belly formed by the fusion of the ventral fins. It can grow up to twelve or more inches in length, but one does not usually find such large specimens on the shore. In these older lumpsuckers the sides of the body have rows of hard knobs which are not present in the young fish. During the breeding season the belly of the male fish becomes pink or red while the female is a dark blue colour. In spring the female lays clumps of pink eggs near low tide, usually in a slight hollow in the beach and these are carefully guarded by the male. Even when attacked by herring gulls the male lumpsucker remains by the eggs and is often killed in so doing.

Many of these fishes have rather peculiar shapes, and the thickset spiny ones like Father Lasher are really ugly, but there are some very attractive creatures among them, and many of them live well in small aquaria. Perhaps the best for this purpose

Fishes of the Seashore

are the wrasses, blennies and gobies. The smaller wrasses, and especially Jago's goldsinny, are very satisfactory for aquaria because they swim about in mid-water. The blennies and gobies, on the other hand, tend to seek the shelter of the rocks and stones and will move by darting from one hiding place to the next.

Shore fishes have varied nesting habits and in this respect they resemble birds. You will find this when you have seen the seaweed nests of stickleback, the empty shell type of nest of the butterfish, and the sand hole in which the female sand goby lays her eggs. Then there are the pipe-fishes with the father looking after the brood, and the eel-pout in which there is no laying of eggs, the young developing within the body of the female.

5. Cliff and Shore Birds

At times the Solan's wing,
As if to show its majesty of strength,
Brushed near us with a roughly winnowing noise.
DAVID MACBETH MOIR in *The Bass Rock*

THE birds of the shore and coast have been the subject of much study, and many books have been written about them. Rightly so, for not only are they beautiful in themselves, but they have interesting habits and life histories, and the calls of many have become an intrinsic part of the seaside. The present chapter is not intended as a full description of the maritime birds, but rather to give some account of how the more common sea birds fit into the scheme of life on the shore. The time has gone when the bird watcher was content merely to name and list the birds seen. How much more interesting it is to know the food of each bird, its enemies, how it competes with other birds for nest sites, and all the details of egg-laying, and the hatching and rearing of the young chicks.

Most of the gulls, terns, cormorants and auks can be identified after a little practice. Perhaps the waders such as sandpipers, dunlins and turnstone are a little more difficult, and you really need a good pair of field glasses so that they can be watched with care from a distance. Fortunately there are a number of

Cliff and Shore Birds

excellent modern books which give the distinguishing characters of birds in a concise way. The most practical of these are James Fisher's Pelican books *Bird Recognition* (sea birds and waders are in Volume 1), and Richard Fitter's *Pocket Guide to British Birds.*

There is no hard and fast boundary between land birds and sea birds. Along rocky coasts blackbirds, rock pipits and wrens are often very common, and ravens are quite normal cliff-breeders. On some cliffs in Cornwall the chough, a crow with red beak and legs occurs in small numbers. But there are certain birds which are nearly always associated with the shore and coast, either for breeding or feeding or both. These are perhaps best discussed by grouping them into (1) the gulls, terns and skuas, (2) the petrels and shearwaters, (3) the waders, (4) the auks, and (5) the cormorants and the gannet.

Of the seagulls the most common are the Herring gull and Lesser black-backed gull, and once they have been recognized it is not difficult to get to know the other species. The Herring gull (Figure 38) is a large bird, grey on the back and on the upper parts of the wings and white elsewhere, except for the wing tips which are black, marked with white. In the adult the bill is yellow with a red spot on the side, and the legs are flesh-coloured. The Lesser black-backed gull (Figure 38) is the same size and build as the Herring gull, but the back and upper parts of the wings are dark slate-grey, and both the bill and legs are yellow. Both these gulls take two to three years to become mature, and during this time they have a juvenile plumage in which the feathers of the whole body are barred brown and white, giving the birds a mottled appearance. In this stage it is not really possible to distinguish between these two gulls with any certainty.

The Great black-backed gull (Figure 38) is distinctly larger

60

FIGURE 38

HERRING GULL

Grey back, wing tips black with white markings. Rest of body white. Bill yellow with red spot on side. Legs flesh-coloured.
Common Gull is smaller and slighter, wings projecting further beyond tail. Bill and legs greenish-yellow. No red spot on bill.

LESSER BLACK-BACKED GULL

Same size as Herring gull. Back and upper parts of wings dark grey, almost black. Bill and legs yellow. Young (immature) birds of this species and of Herring gull and Common gull have mottled brownish plumage.

GREAT BLACK-BACKED GULL

Powerful build, larger than Herring gull. Plumage as in Lesser black-backed gull but blacker. Bill yellow. Legs flesh coloured. Immature birds with mottled plumage.

than the Herring or Lesser black-backed gulls and gives the appearance of great power. Its plumage is about the same as that of the Lesser black-back, and it also has a yellow bill, but the legs are flesh-coloured or almost white. As a young bird it has the mottled plumage but even at this age it is a larger, tougher looking bird than the Herring and Lesser black-backed gulls.

The Common gull is badly named, being by no means as common and widespread as some of the other seagulls. It is a little smaller than the Herring gull, with similar plumage (grey above, white below), but it differs in that the wings project further beyond the tail, the bill is slighter, and the whole bird has a more slender appearance. The bill and legs are greenish-yellow, and there is no red spot on the side of the bill.

The Kittiwake, the most attractive of all the gulls, is smaller again than the Common gull. Most of its plumage is the same in colour, except that the wing tips are black without any white. The legs are brownish-black, there are only three toes on each foot, whereas in the other gulls there are four. The young Kittiwake does not have a mottled plumage, but during the first winter of its life it has a black ring across the neck and also across the wing, and a small dark patch of feathers behind the eyes.

The Black-headed gull is another small gull, not quite as large as a Kittiwake, and very common in certain areas especially in the north of England. Many of its breeding colonies are quite far inland. It has a chocolate-brown, almost black head in summer, but in winter it loses the dark head feathers, and until the following spring the head is white, except for a small dark area behind the eyes. The wings are black-tipped and the bill and legs are red.

For graceful flying there are few birds which can rival the terns, which have long slender wings and the grey and white

Cliff and Shore Birds

plumage of the Kittiwake, but they are not so beautiful on land as the legs are rather short. In summer the Common Tern has a red bill with a black tip, but in winter most of the red is lost. In the Arctic Tern the bill is all red in summer, and pure black in winter, and its legs are even shorter than those of the Common Tern. Both these birds nest in colonies on sand and shingle, and also on flat ground at the tops of cliffs, the nest being only a shallow dip in the ground, sometimes with a few wisps of grass. The Common Tern breeds in many places along the coasts of Britain, but colonies have not been recorded from the Yorkshire coast, Bristol Channel or south Devon. The Arctic Tern is by no means restricted to the Arctic and it breeds along the north and west coasts of Scotland, in Anglesey and in the Isle of Man. Terns have a nasty habit of diving on you when you walk through their colony. Normally they do not touch your head, but I have known blood to appear where a tern's bill has just scraped a bald head.

Terns feed by flying down and skimming small fish and crustaceans from near the surface of the sea. Gulls, on the other hand, feed on more or less anything that is available. They will follow ships at sea where they eat the scraps thrown out from the galley, and one of the best sights is a flock of gulls following a trawler, especially when the fishermen are cleaning up after bringing a trawl haul aboard. On the shore gulls feed on dead or dying animals of all sorts as well as on insects, potatoes, apples, corn and other seeds. In fact they are the scavengers of the shore. In the middle of the last century there were few or no records of gulls feeding and roosting inland, but nowadays Herring gulls and Black-headed gulls are commonly seen far inland on farms and moorland.

When a seagull or skua eats another bird or a small rabbit, it swallows more or less the whole animal which passes from its

Cliff and Shore Birds

mouth to the crop (which comes before the main stomach). The crop has hard muscular walls which grind up the food. In this process the indigestible fur, feathers and bones are separated from the soft parts, which are passed down to the stomach. The hard parts are kept in the crop, where they are pressed into a pellet and from time to time the bird coughs up these pellets, and you will probably find them on rocks where gulls sit out during the day. Incidentally, bird pellets are not confined to sea birds and you will often see them at the foot of a tree which an owl has used as a perch.

Gulls and terns are gentle in their habits compared with the skuas—gull-like birds with dull dark brown feathers in place of the clean greys and blacks of the gulls. Skuas are the chief robbers of the shore. While the gulls merely search out the dead and the dying and the stinking carrion, skuas feed by chasing gulls, terns, puffins and guillemots and making them disgorge their food which they then catch in mid-air. In this they show a great deal of flying skill, twisting and turning somewhat in the same way as the hawks do on land. They also feed on fish and small sea animals which they catch themselves.

The Arctic Skua has brown upperparts, and an unmistakable tail, which has the central feathers longer than the side feathers. You will not often see an Arctic Skua in England, although they have been recorded from most of the coastal areas, but they are more common in Scotland, where they breed in the extreme north, and in the Outer Hebrides, Shetland and the Orkneys.

The Great Skua is a larger bird, between a Herring gull and a Great black-backed gull in size, but with dark brown plumage and dark legs and bill. There is a white patch near the front edge of the wing, best seen when the bird is in flight—in fact the photograph (Plate 1) was taken from the deck of a ship, looking down on a Great Skua which was flying by close to the surface of the sea. Great Skuas breed in Orkney and Shetland (where they are known as bonxies), and also further north in Iceland and the Faeroes. They are not often seen on the mainland of Britain except in winter when they travel south. They feed like the Arctic Skua, but being larger they are also bolder and will catch and eat young gulls and puffins.

The petrels and shearwaters are more birds of the ocean than of the shore, and they often spend long periods at sea. In fact some of them, such as the Manx shearwater, are rarely seen near the land, except in the neighbourhood of their nests, and even these they only enter and leave in twilight or darkness. Manx shearwaters breed in colonies on islands off the coast, and the nest is made in a burrow which the birds dig out themselves. R. M. Lockley has made a long and careful study of these birds, and his fine book *Shearwaters* is well worth reading. He found that the egg was incubated for about 54 days—a domestic hen's egg hatches in 21 days—and that the chick was then fed by the parent once every night for 8½ weeks. About the sixtieth day from hatching the chick was deserted by the parents and it then remained in its burrow, without any food, for about a fortnight, before leaving and finding its own way down to the sea. This is a very long period for a young bird to stay in the nest.

Shearwaters make a low grunting noise when they are in the nests at night, and so do storm petrels—delicate soot-coloured birds which nest in holes in walls and banks. The grunts of a colony of storm petrels can be alarming on a dark still night. There is usually a peculiar musky smell around their nests—a smell which is characteristic of all petrels and shearwaters.

The fulmar is a large grey and white bird, very graceful in flight, often mistaken for a gull, from which it can easily be distinguished by its much longer wings and the well-defined tube-like nostrils which run along the edge of the upper part of the

Cliff and Shore Birds

bill. Storm petrels and shearwaters also have these prominent nostrils. Fulmars nest in colonies, but always in the open, and usually on wide comfortable ledges on cliffs. They breed now all round the coast of Scotland, and in western Ireland, but only here and there in the southern half of Britain, (for example on the coast of south-west Wales, Lundy Island in the Bristol Channel, the Scilly Isles and Cornwall). At the beginning of the nineteenth century the fulmar bred in Britain only at St. Kilda, forty miles west of the Hebrides, but since that time it has spread enormously both to the north and south. The story of this spread has been told by James Fisher in his interesting book *The Fulmar*, which is certainly one of the most complete and thorough books ever written on a single species of bird.

Fulmars feed on small plankton animals, on dead fish and birds, and also on the decaying remains of seals and whales. That is why one sees flocks of them in the waters near whaling stations, where they pick up bits of whale offal and blubber. They have an unpleasant habit of ejecting an evil-smelling, musky oil when they are scared. This oil seems to scent their own feathers permanently, and one has to be very tired to enjoy a night's sleep in a feather bed made from the pluckings of a fulmar. If you should be unfortunate enough to be hit by a jet of fulmar oil there is little you can do to get your clothing clean, unless you have a wide variety of chemical cleaning agents.

Normally fulmars lay only one egg which takes seven to eight weeks to hatch. You will remember those attractive pictures of the chicks of small woodland birds, sitting up in their nests, waiting for a parent bird to drop fat caterpillars into their gaping mouths. The feeding of a fulmar chick is not at all like that. The fulmar chick puts its beak or sometimes its whole head into the parent's mouth, and is fed on a revolting oily soup, which the parent bird regurgitates from its own crop. As these meals go on for about seven weeks it is not surprising that the chick soon resembles a cartoonist's model in its oily grossness. The word 'fulmar' is derived directly from the Old Norse for 'foul gull'.

FIGURE 39

Oystercatcher

The oystercatcher (Figure 39) is an attractive bird which breeds on nearly all parts of our coasts and is perhaps the most distinctive of the waders. It has a black back and head, and white underparts, with an orange bill and pink legs. The call is a loud piping sound. Although oystercatchers can open and eat oysters they feed mainly on mussels. These they open by striking the shells on a stone, and either breaking them or shifting the two valves so that they can insert their long powerful beaks.

Much smaller than the oystercatcher is the ringed plover which has a characteristic white ring round the neck, and below this an almost black band round the upper part of the breast. Ringed plovers are seen in all the coastal districts of Britain and also at many places inland. They feed on sandy and muddy shores, picking up sandhoppers and small marine worms, such as ragworms, and on drier ground they take insects. The dunlin is another small wader, about the same size as the ringed plover but with a longer black bill. This long bill enables them to probe deep into the wet mud and sand, and thus find worms and small sandhoppers of types which live buried. They breed in Scotland and northern England, and also in Devon and parts of Wales.

The dunlin is only one of a large number of long-billed waders which appear on our shores from time to time. Many of these birds do not nest in Britain, but are seen here in spring and autumn as they travel to and from their northern breeding grounds. Turnstone, knot, purple sandpiper, whimbrel and sanderling do this, and can often be seen at these seasons feeding on sandy and muddy shores. Turnstones feed by turning over

FIGURE 40

Puffin

small stones and picking up animals—sand-hoppers, small mussels and limpets. Sometimes if a stone is large two or three

I. Great Skua, seen from above, flying along above the surface of the sea.

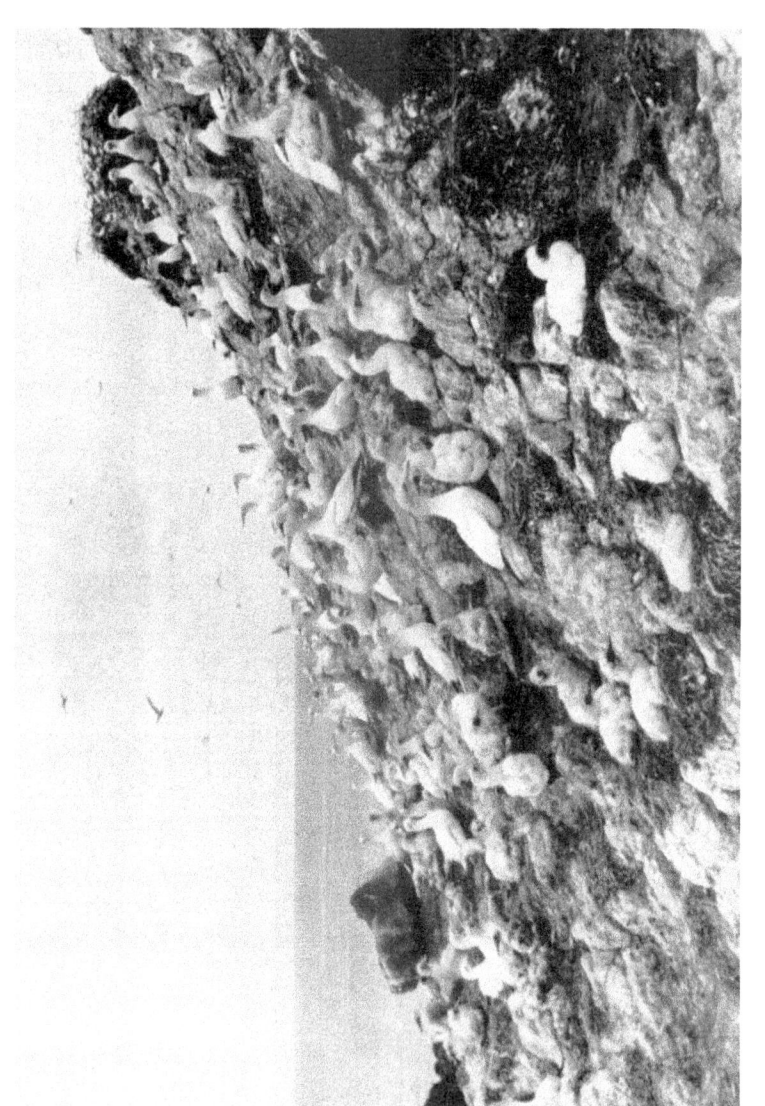

II. Part of a gannet colony, showing parent birds and young.

III. Part of the gannet colony, on Ailsa Craig.

IV. A group of dahlia sea anemones (photograph, D. P. Wilson).

turnstones will put their bills under one side of it and will then lift it over together.

The auks are an interesting group of seabirds, with black and white plumage, and they are usually seen on steep rocky coastlines and especially on high cliffs. They include puffins, razorbills and guillemots. There is no need to describe a puffin (Figure 40), for there is really no other bird with which it is likely to be confused. The fantastic bill is coloured yellow and red with blue markings in summer, but in winter it is less gaudy, being merely brown and orange. Puffins nest in holes in rocks or in burrows in those grassy slopes which are so common both above and below steep cliffs. Often the nest may be in an empty rabbit hole. Their breeding colonies are commoner in the north of Scotland than elsewhere in Britain, but they do also nest in south-west Scotland, Wales and along the north coast of Devon and Cornwall.

Puffins dive for their food, and can stay under water for about half a minute, and while doing so they are swimming with their wings. They feed on plankton animals and fish, and during the nesting season they can be seen returning to their nest carrying six to twelve little fish, all neatly arranged crosswise between the blades of the bill. I have never understood how they manage to catch the last of these fish without losing the first. In the Faeroe Islands, where there are many puffin colonies, thousands of the birds are caught every year and either eaten fresh or stored away in salt for the winter. They are excellent eating—not at all fishy.

The razorbill is larger than the puffin and has a black bill, with white cross-markings. It breeds on cliffs, sometimes on ledges in the open, but more often in sheltered holes in the rock. It feeds in the same way as the puffin and makes the same sort of grunting noise when it is on the nest. The third member of the auk family is the guillemot, which has a dark chocolate-brown back and head, and white underparts. In winter the head is lighter in colour, especially the cheeks which are white. The bill is pointed and black and much lighter in build than that of the razorbill. Guillemots nest on open cliff ledges, often quite narrow ones, and on top of rock pinnacles and stacks. They are attractive birds to watch but you need a pair of field glasses, as the nests are usually difficult to approach. Most of the colonies of guillemots are again in the north—Scotland, Orkney, Shetland, Faeroes, Iceland and south Greenland. However, there are also colonies in the Isle of Man, south-west Wales, Cornwall, Dorset and Devon, including one at Berry Head near Torquay.

Pure white, with black-tipped wings spanning six feet. Such is the gannet, known as the solan goose in Scotland, the most handsome of all our sea birds. It nests on the broader cliff ledges (Plate III) leaving the narrower ledges for guillemots and kitti-wakes. In 1936 James Fisher and I started studying the gannets at the breeding colony on Ailsa Craig in the Firth of Clyde (*see* Plate III). Here the gannets nest on a long range of almost vertical cliffs on the western side of the island. In the years following we moved to many other islands in search of the cliff colonies of the gannet—to the Bass Rock, St. Kilda, Sula Sgeir off north-west Scotland, Noss in Shetland, the Faeroe Islands and Iceland.

The main purpose of this work was to find out the numbers of breeding gannets in each colony. We were able to attempt this because, unlike the gulls and terns which nest in many small straggly colonies along the coast, the gannet breeds only in a small number of large colonies. In 1939 there were twenty-two such colonies of the gannet, twelve in Britain, one in the Faeroe Islands, three in Iceland and six in the Gulf of St. Lawrence, in Canada. With the help of a team of observers we were able to count the numbers of breeding gannets on all these colonies

Cliff and Shore Birds

except for four in the Canadian area, for which we obtained estimates. We found there were about 70,000 pairs of nesting gannets at the seventeen colonies in Britain, Ireland, the Faeroes and Iceland, and about 12,000 at the colonies in Canada. In 1949 the counts at the Eastern Atlantic colonies were repeated and it was found that the numbers had risen from 70,000 to 82,000 pairs. The number of colonies had also increased, and there were twenty-three colonies on this side of the Atlantic Ocean.

The gannet is one of the few animals of which we have a reasonably good idea of the total population, and with these two censuses as a basis we can now follow the ups and downs of its numbers in the years to come.

Gannets are very strong fliers, but are not so good at coming in to land, especially when they have to land on a cliff ledge. On Ailsa Craig after a storm we often found gannets floundering about among the boulders at the foot of the cliffs. These birds had all broken a wing in attempting to land. Out at sea they are safe in all weathers, and there you see them diving for fish, mostly herring, pollack, whiting and mackerel. They start the dive with the wings half open like a swept-wing aircraft. Just as they are about to enter the water they close the wings alongside their bodies so that when they strike the surface they have the shape of a torpedo. They mostly dive from twenty to forty feet above the surface, and they have been caught quite deep down in fishermen's nets. Gannets usually fish out at sea some miles from the colony, but this depends on the position of the fish shoals and I have seen them diving at thirty yards from the shore. One winter they were fishing right inside Plymouth Sound close under the Hoe.

Cormorants (Figure 41) and shags are far more birds of the coast than gannets and usually nest on low-lying offshore rocks and skerries. They also dive for food but not so gracefully and

71

FIGURE 41

Cormorant

not from any great height. They sometimes feed on small cod and herring, but a great deal of their food consists of shallow-water fish, such as wrasse, grey mullet, blennies, flounders, sand eels and sea sticklebacks.

It seems that gulls and perhaps some of the waders can tolerate the presence of human beings, for you can see them feeding along almost every part of the coast, even on the shores in front of sea-side towns. Petrels, shearwaters, razorbills, puffins, and gannets, on the other hand, are birds of the outlying coasts. In search of them you will experience the very real fascination of islands,

Cliff and Shore Birds

which appeal not only because of the bird colonies which they may contain, but also for many other things—rabbit-browsed springy turf near the summit, small lochs hidden away in sheltered valleys, and perhaps a shore broken up by inlets with caves into which all manner of odds and ends may drift with the tide.

6. Crabs, Lobsters, Prawns and Barnacles

For all the ingenious men, and all the scientific men, and all the fanciful men, in the world, with all the old German bogey-painters into the bargain, could never invent, if all their wits were boiled into one, anything so curious, and so ridiculous, as a lobster.

CHARLES KINGSLEY in *The Water Babies*

FOR prawn hunting in the summer the best dress is a bathing costume, so that you can explore the large rock pools and cave pools where the water may be six feet or more deep, and where there are plenty of prawns. You find these pools along the coasts of Devon and Cornwall, in south-west Wales, and in the west of Scotland. Only visit them at low tide when there is no danger of being cut off. Never go alone. Shrimps (Figure 42) are grey-brown in colour and usually prefer flat, open sandy places. You will find them most easily in those shallow pools which are left in the sand when the tide goes out. For shrimping you need a net with a straight leading edge which can be pushed slowly along the sand, but for prawning the net is better with a rounded point which can get into awkward places in rock pools.

Prawns are almost transparent when living and they only go pink when they are cooked. The body of a prawn is covered by

Crabs, Lobsters, Prawns and Barnacles

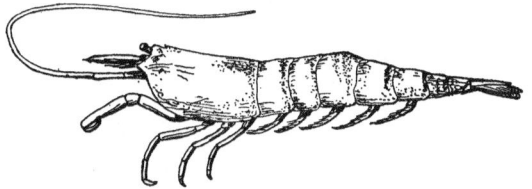

FIGURE 42

Shrimp. Only the limbs of the left side are shown (three-quarters natural size)

hard horny plates, and the many-jointed legs are also enclosed by the same sort of casing. In front of the ordinary walking legs there is a pair of limbs armed with small pincers (Figure 43). A prawn can move in two ways, either by walking forwards on

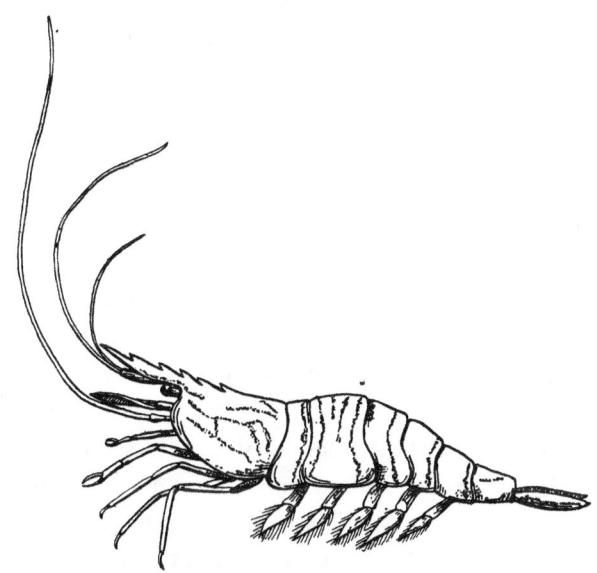

FIGURE 43

Prawn. Only the limbs of the left side are shown (three-quarters natural size)

75

the tips of the legs like a ballet dancer, or it can move backwards and much faster by giving a strong flip with its tail.

Animals built in the same way as the prawn, with a hard outer crusty skeleton and jointed limbs are known as the crustaceans; most of them live in the sea or on the shore (crabs, lobsters, prawns, shrimps and sandhoppers), but there are some which live in fresh water and others like the wood lice and slaters which live in damp places on land. You will see that the eyes of crabs, lobsters and prawns are raised on short stalks which can move slightly.

Lobsters are not found very often on the shore, but you can see them in fishing villages for they are caught by the fishermen in baited lobster pots set in deeper water. They are coloured dark blue when living but turn red when boiled for eating. On the coasts of Devon and Cornwall fishermen often bring in spiny lobsters or crawfish (the *langouste* of the French), which have no large pincers and are coloured red-brown when living; they have a very spiny outer covering.

The outer casing of a lobster is, of course, much harder than that of a prawn, for it is strengthened by deposits of lime. This skeleton is like the coat of armour of a medieval knight, and is a good protection against enemies. But it cannot expand as the animal grows, and so when they are ready to grow, lobsters and other crustaceans lose their covering by a moult. At each moult the casing splits across the middle of the back and the animal draws itself out of the two halves of the old shell. Once it has struggled free from the shell its body is quite soft and it is at this stage that it really grows. The actual growing period is quite short, usually only a few hours, and one can almost see the lobster swelling. As soon as this is over the outer skin begins to harden, and in a few days the new skeleton of the body and legs is as hard as the old one. When they are in the soft state, before

76

Crabs, Lobsters, Prawns and Barnacles

the new shell skeleton has hardened, lobsters, crabs and prawns are often attacked by animals which could not normally harm them when their body coverings are hard. I have occasionally found soft crabs on the shore, hiding under rocks, but the best place to watch a moulting crab is in an aquarium. There you are not worried by the return of the tide and you can touch the crab every now and again and feel how the soft leathery skin hardens into the new limy outer crust.

Crabs on the shore have a short squat body, with a pair of strong pincers, the whole animal being broader than it is long. A look at the jointing of the legs will help explain how crabs manage to walk sideways so successfully. The common shore

FIGURE 44
Common shore crab (one-half natural size)

crab (Figure 44) is found everywhere between tide marks, usually sheltering beneath stones. They spend a large part of their time out of water, in fact we find that it is not easy to keep

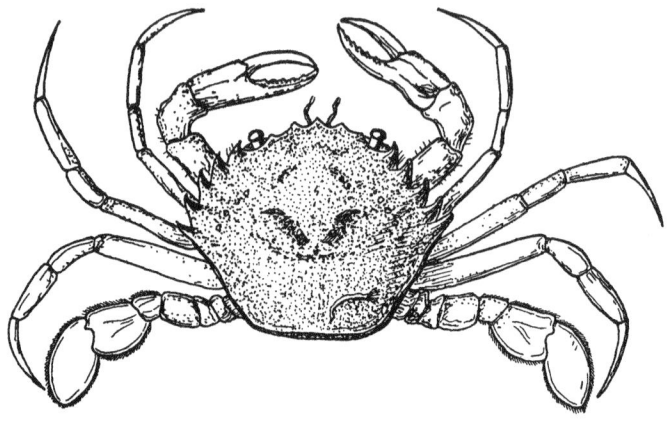

FIGURE 45

Swimming crab, taken from offshore. Note the back pair of legs form
paddles for swimming (one-half natural size)

them alive in an aquarium unless they can climb out of the
water for part of the day.

Edible crabs are much larger and their pincers are more
powerful than those of shore crabs and they are usually found in
deeper water offshore where they are caught by fishermen in
baited pots in the same way as lobsters. The graceful swimming
crab (Figure 45), so different in its movements from the shore
crab, is also common below low tide. Swimming crabs swim
sideways using the last pair of legs which have broad paddle
ends.

Hermit crabs (Figure 46) are in some ways intermediate
between lobsters and crabs in appearance, but the tail end of the
body does not have a hard outer skeleton. Instead they get all
the protection they need by living inside empty winkle or whelk
shells. The hermit crab clings on to the inside of the empty shell
by means of the tiny legs on the tail end, while the front part of
the body, with the walking legs and pincers, protrudes from the

Crabs, Lobsters, Prawns and Barnacles

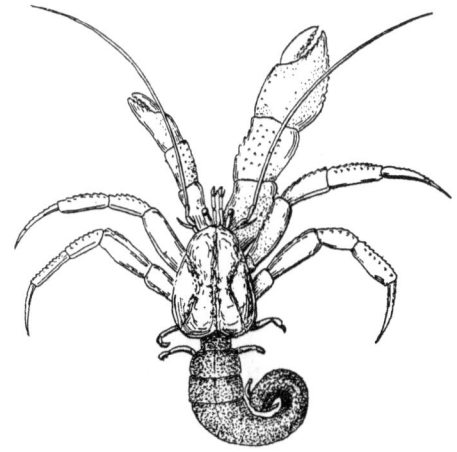

FIGURE 46

Hermit crab. One of the large hermits as it appears when taken out of its protecting whelk shell. The tiny limbs at the back end of the body help to hold the animal in the shell (one-half natural size)

mouth of the shell. In this way they are able to walk about dragging their shell house with them while they hunt for food, and, if in danger they can withdraw completely, pincers, legs and all, into the safety of the hard shell. When a hermit crab has grown too large for its shell, it finds a larger one, uncoils its tail end from the old shell, and quickly moves tail first into the new shell. These are attractive creatures, and are not difficult to keep

FIGURE 47

Porcelain crab. Common under stones on the shore (two-thirds natural size)

Crabs, Lobsters, Prawns and Barnacles

in a small aquarium where you can feed them with small pieces of fish. There is another little crab, the porcelain crab (Figure 47) which lives under rocks and among seaweeds between tidemarks. It is easily known by the enormous size of the pincers compared with the rest of the body.

Under the long drifts of dead seaweed at high water mark on a sandy shore there live enormous numbers of sandhoppers (Figure 48), which are also crustaceans. They can jump or hop

FIGURE 48
Sandhopper (twice natural size)

for quite long distances if the seaweed above them is disturbed. At the beginning of a jump the tail end is bent under the rest of the body and the animal jumps by very quickly straightening its body, using its back legs to get a hold on the sand. Sandhoppers live by browsing on the rotting seaweed, breaking it up with

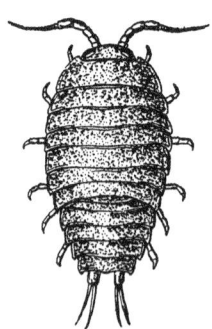

FIGURE 49
Sea slater (natural size)
80

their tiny mouthparts. Sea slaters (Figure 49) are often found in rock pools climbing about among the wrack weeds, on which they feed; they look like large wood lice.

Perhaps the most peculiar of all crustaceans are the barnacles. Up to about 120 years ago they were looked upon as molluscs like snails and cockles, partly because of the limy plates in which they are encased. We now know that they begin their life by hatching out of eggs as microscopic larvae, each with one eye and a few limbs (Figure 50*a*), and that for some days these larvae swim around freely in the sea, grow more limbs and

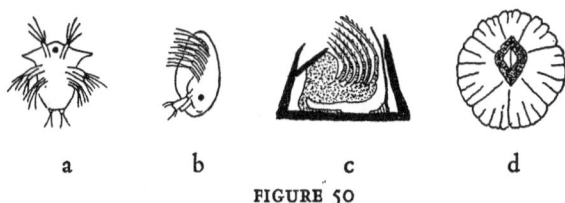

a   b   c   d

FIGURE 50

Life history of the barnacle:
- (*a*) Nauplius stage. With one eye and three pairs of legs; this stage moults to form
- (*b*) the cypris stage, with two eyes and six pairs of legs. This stage settles down on a rock, attaches itself by its antennae and forms shelly plates, and is then an adult barnacle
- (*c*) Section through an adult barnacle, showing the shell (black) and the animal (dotted)
- (*d*) Adult barnacle seen from above

develop a pair of eyes in addition to the single tiny eye which was there when they hatched (Figure 50*b*). Then they sink to the bottom where they attach themselves to rocks or anything firm. In doing this they literally stand on their heads, which become cemented to the rock. This amazing change from active swimming larvae to fixed barnacles was first observed about 1823 by a British Army surgeon, John Vaughan Thompson, who was working at Cork in the south of Ireland. Thompson caught

Crabs, Lobsters, Prawns and Barnacles

some of the larvae in a fine muslin net—he was also the first to use a fine mesh net for collecting these tiny floating animals—and kept them in a bowl of sea-water. He wrote: '. . . they were taken on May 1st, and on the night of the 8th, the author had the satisfaction to find that two of them had thrown off their exuvia,[1] and wonderful to say, were firmly adhering to the bottom of the vessel and changed into young Barnacles! such as are usually seen intermixed with grown specimens on rocks and stones at this season of the year'.

As the fixed barnacles grow they form six protective limy plates round their body, and at the top end of the plates, which is really the tail end of the animal, there is an opening (Figure 50c). When the tide is in and the barnacle is covered with water the legs are pushed out through this opening to scoop through the water like a net. This is how the barnacle feeds, for the long hairy legs make an excellent net for catching tiny floating animals and plants. You can watch this interesting method of feeding if you put a piece of barnacle-covered stone in a dish of sea-water. Be sure not to jog the dish and in a few minutes you will see the feathery legs of the barnacle coming out.

Besides the small tent-shaped barnacles (Figure 50d) found everywhere on the shore you may come across a piece of timber covered with goose barnacles (Figure 51). These are very handsome animals with polished whitish plates, and a tough flexible stalk between the body and the timber to which they are attached. For hundreds of years there was a curious belief that these stalked goose barnacles were really the young of the bird which has become known as the barnacle goose. In 1187 Gerald of Wales, after a tour in Ireland, wrote: 'There are in this place many birds which are called Bernacae; Nature produces them against Nature in the most extraordinary way. They are

[1] Had moulted their skeletons.

82

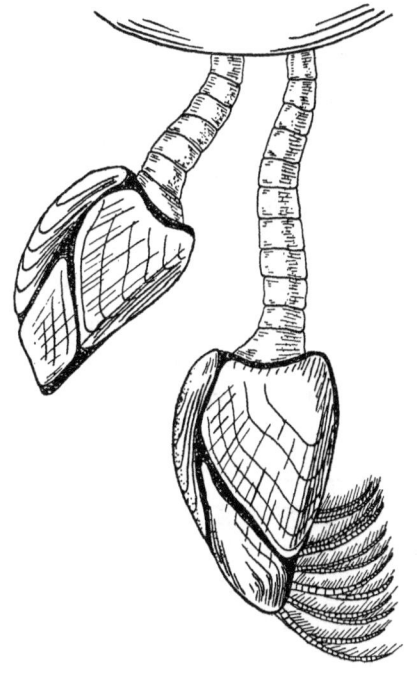

FIGURE 51

Goose barnacles hanging from a fisherman's glass buoy. The goose
barnacle on the right shows the hairy legs which form a scoop net
for catching food (about natural size)

like marsh geese but somewhat smaller. They are produced from
fir timber tossed along the sea, and are at first like gum. Afterwards they hang down by their beaks as if they were a seaweed
attached to the timber, and are surrounded by shells in order to
grow more freely. Having thus in process of time been clothed
with a strong coat of feathers, they either fall into the water or
fly freely away into the air. They derive their food and growth
from the sap of the wood or from the sea, by a secret and most
wonderful process of alimentation. I have frequently seen, with
my own eyes, more than a thousand of these small bodies of

birds, hanging down on the seashore from one piece of timber, enclosed in their shells, and already formed."

There have been many versions of this weird and untrue story and in one the pieces of timber came to be described as living trees, for in Gerard's *Herball* (1597) there is a passage which reads: 'There are found in the north parts of Scotland and the islands adjacent, called Orchades, certaine trees whereon do grow certaine shells of a white colour tending to russet, wherein are contained little living creatures: which shells in time of maturity doe open, and out of them grow those little living things which, falling into the water, doe become fowles, which we call barnacles. . . .'

There is, of course, a certain similarity between the feathers of a bird and the long sweeping legs of a barnacle, and the story conveniently filled a gap in our ancestor's knowledge of the barnacle goose, for this bird only appears in Britain in winter and nobody had seen it nesting. This was not surprising for it only breeds north of the Arctic Circle in Spitsbergen and east Greenland. There is, therefore, no real connection between the goose barnacle (a crustacean) and the barnacle goose.

There are many different kinds of tiny crustaceans swimming and floating about in the waters of the sea. Most of these are only just visible as specks to the naked eye, but under the microscope you can see that they are perfect little crustaceans, each with jointed legs and an outer skeleton.

These smaller crustaceans are part of the seas' floating population, usually known as the plankton, and they form an important food supply for small fishes. Some crustaceans in the plankton are adult animals like the copepod in Figure 52a which never grow any larger, but many are just the young stages of animals which live as adults on the shore or on the sea bottom in deeper water. Figure 52*b* shows one of these young stages, an early larva of the common shore crab, a weird looking creature quite unlike the adult crab. These tiny larvae hatch out from the

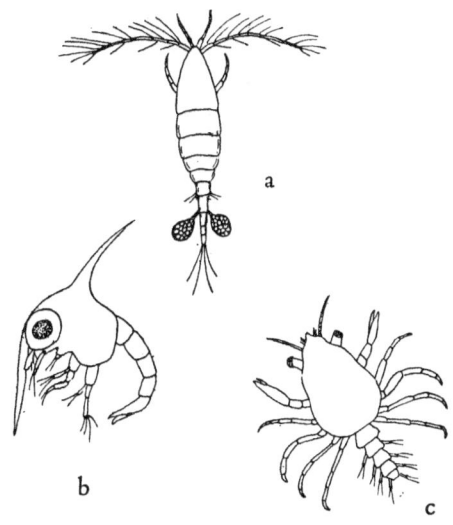

FIGURE 52

Three animals of the plankton, greatly enlarged:
    (*a*) a copepod crustacean
    (*b*) a zooea larva, the early stage of the common shore crab
    (*c*) a megalopa larva, a later stage of the common shore crab, before it
          moults to the adult stage

eggs which the mother crab carries around on the underside of her body. Actually the eggs are attached to the tail of the body which is kept folded away so neatly in the crab, and looks as though it is hinged to the rest of the body. In the lobster and prawn these egg masses are more obvious because the tail is so large, and also in the lobster the eggs are coloured bright green. Crustaceans carrying eggs in this way are said to be 'in berry' or

Crabs, Lobsters, Prawns and Barnacles

berried. If you watch a berried prawn in an aquarium you will see that she keeps the water moving over her eggs by a continual paddling of her swimmerets—those broad oarshaped limbs which lie under the hind part of the body.

The term 'shellfish' covers a number of edible things and among them some of the most delicious are crustaceans. Crabs, lobsters, crawfish, prawns and shrimps are all shellfish in table talk, and much time and energy is spent in collecting and marketing them. Rightly so, for not only are these animals most enjoyable when properly prepared, but they also happen to have high food values. The other half of the shellfish are found among the molluscs (winkles, whelks, cockles, mussels, octopus and similar animals which form the subject of the next chapter).

7. Winkles, Limpets, Mussels and Cockles

And should the strongest arm endeavour
The limpet from its rock to sever,
'Tis seen its loved support to clasp,
With such tenacity of grasp,
We wonder that such strength should dwell
In such a small and simple shell.

WORDSWORTH

ON every rocky shore you will find limpets, periwinkles, mussels and dog whelks. These are all molluscs, animals with soft bodies, usually protected by some form of shell. I think that we are first attracted by the shells of the molluscs as we walk along the shore, hunting among the rocks and in sandy places. For these shells, even those of some of the common ones, are incredibly beautiful, and for thousands of years they have been prized by Man. The shells of some large snail-like molluscs from tropical beaches fetch a high price when they are in good condition. In some parts of the world shells have been used as a form of currency. This applies especially to the money cowries, which are pretty little shells, similar in shape to the cowries found on beaches in Britain.

Mother-of-pearl is obtained from mollusc shells, the best and clearest quality coming from the pearl oyster, which is fished in

Winkles, Limpets, Mussels and Cockles

the East Indies and off northern Australia. The lustrous mother-of-pearl is laid down as the inside layer of the shell and it occurs in some of our British mollusc shells. Pearls are deposits of this lustrous nacre, laid down round a grain of sand or other foreign body which has found its way between the shell and the fleshy mantle of the animal. The mantle is the coat of skin which lines the shell and which actually secretes the shell itself. Most pearls are taken from the pearl oyster. If a tiny sand grain is placed inside a pearl oyster near the mantle, the animal will probably lay down mother-of-pearl round it and eventually a pearl will be formed. This is a cultured pearl. In some of the rivers of Scotland there are freshwater mussels which produce pearls, and at one time there was a considerable trade in them. Pearls have been found in common mussels, scallops and oysters, but only rarely.

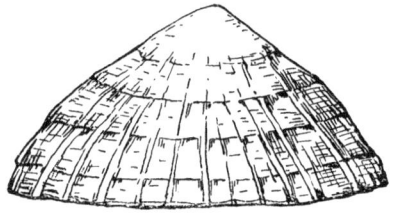

FIGURE 53
Common limpet. The shell seen from the side (natural size)

Limpets (Figure 53) are common all round the coasts of Britain, between tidemarks, and they seem to share the large flat expanses of rocks with the acorn barnacles. When the tide is out limpets are found attached to the rocks so strongly that only a sharp blow with a knife or hammer will move them, but when the tide is in each one moves about freely on its strong muscular toot. This is when they feed by rasping away small seaweeds from the surface of the rock. As the tide starts to go out each

Winkles, Limpets, Mussels and Cockles

limpet returns again to the same spot on the rock, so that in time the edge of the shell wears an almost circular depression in the softer rocks. If you can get a limpet to attach itself to the side of a glass jar you will be able to see the foot by which it clings to hard rocky surfaces.

The blue-rayed limpet is a small mollusc with a shell similar to that of the common limpet, but with a more rounded top. It is about half an inch long and is delicately marked with seven or more radiating blue stripes. They live among the tangle-weeds at low tide, and also among the twisted hold-fasts of these seaweeds, where they eat themselves out a safe sheltered resting place.

Like the limpets the winkles and top-shells crawl on a soft leathery foot, which they can pull back into their spiral shell together with the rest of the body. The true periwinkle (Figure 54) is still much eaten in England, especially in London, and rightly so, for it has an excellent flavour and is tender. Even a

FIGURE 54
Periwinkle (three-quarters natural size)
(a) the animal in its shell, seen from above
(b) the shell from below

hundred years ago the consumption in London was something like 2,000 tons per year. Most of these winkles are eaten plain boiled, with salt and vinegar, but Mr. Lovell in his book *Edible British Mollusca* gives an excellent recipe for periwinkle soup which is well worth trying:

89

Winkles, Limpets, Mussels and Cockles

PERIWINKLE SOUP—Take a pint and a half or a quart of periwinkles, wash them well, and boil them in a saucepan with a handful or two of salt, to enable you to pick out the fish easily. Put a little dripping or butter into a saucepan, with an onion or carrot, some chopped parsley, and a sprig of thyme, and fry until it become brown. Add a pint of water to this, and as soon as it boils put in the periwinkles (which have been previously picked out of their shells), with a little pepper and salt, and let the whole boil again for half an hour.

There are four or five different winkles on the shore but the largest one, to which this recipe refers, is found most commonly down near low water. It has a strong brownish shell (Figure 54), sometimes marked with lighter bands. They feed when the tide is in, browsing on the small slimy weeds which cover the rocks, and when the tide goes out they crawl under stones and weeds for shelter from sun, rain and wind. Further up the shore, among the knotted wrack you will find a zone of the dwarf winkle (Figure 55) which has a brown or bright yellow shell, with a

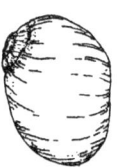

FIGURE 55
Dwarf winkle, usually coloured brown or yellow (natural size)

rounded peak. Near high-water mark there is a third, much smaller winkle, with a sharply peaked brown shell.

The top shells are vegetarian feeders like the periwinkles, but they have much finer shells with attractive markings. The commonest top-shell is very abundant, especially in southern England

and is often found together with a second kind of top-shell, *Gibbula umbilicalis*, which has broader darker markings. In both these animals the shell is flattened, but in another species (Figure 56) the spire of the shell is tall, cone-shaped, and pointed, and

FIGURE 56

A top-shell, with the animal, seen from the side (three-quarters natural size)

the red and yellow marbled patterning make it one of the most beautiful shore animals. It is not uncommon on the shore in southern England, and also on the west coast, but in the east it is usually only dredged up from deeper water.

The winkles, top-shells and limpets are all plant eaters, but the dog whelk feeds on animal flesh, and the common whelk and netted dog whelk feed on carrion (dead animals). The common whelk (Figure 57), known in Scotland as the buckie, is a large animal, with a shell up to four or five inches long. Whelks lay their eggs in large characteristic masses (Figure 57) which are cemented to rocks. Each horny egg case is flat, golden in colour, and contains a single egg. Out of the eggs hatch tiny but complete young whelks, which crawl off leaving the empty egg cases which lose their golden colour and are afterwards often found washed up on the beach. The young whelks are cannibals and they eat up their neighbours as soon as they have hatched so that very few whelks survive from each egg mass. The flesh of the whelk is sometimes used as a bait for crabs and lobsters, and

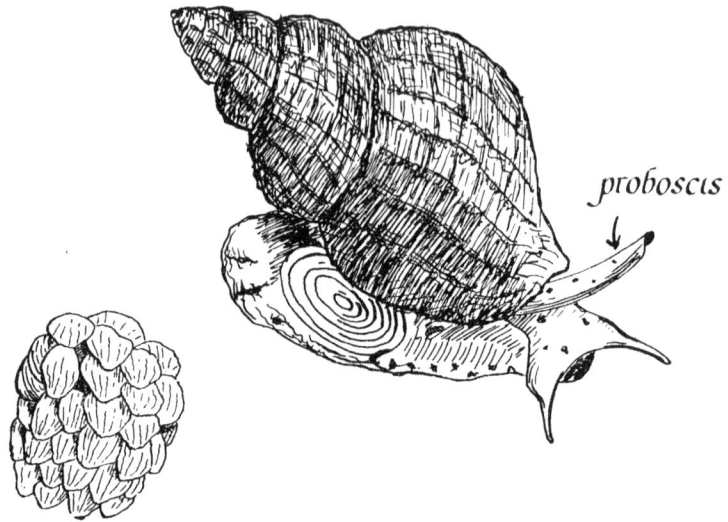

FIGURE 57

Common whelk, and its egg mass (three-quarters natural size)

also for baiting long lines for cod. Whelks can be eaten boiled, but they are tough, and I have always found the flavour to be rather unpleasant.

The dog whelk (Figure 58) is a much smaller animal, common on rocks among winkles and top-shells. Most of the shells are

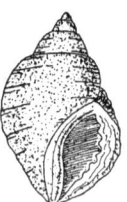

FIGURE 58

Dog whelk shell (three-quarters natural size)

white or brown, but some are yellowish, or they may even be

Winkles, Limpets, Mussels and Cockles

banded brown and white. The dog whelk has a tiny gland in its mantle, the contents of which turn purple on exposure to the air. This purple pigment was much used in ancient times as a dye for the robes of the Roman emperors—in fact it gave the original Imperial Purple. Dog whelks feed on other molluscs and on barnacles. These they attack by boring a hole in their shell with the proboscis, and then sucking out the soft parts of the prey.

The netted dog whelk is also common on the shore and is easily recognized by the surface of the shell being marked by ridges which divide it up into small square patches. Figure 59

FIGURE 59
Netted dog whelk (three-quarters natural size)

shows the animal in its shell with the long snout sticking out in front.

Limpets, winkles, whelks and top-shells are all animals which have a single spiral shell protecting their body, but there are other molluscs, like the mussel and cockle, which have two shells, hinged together at the top edge. Figure 61 shows the position of a cockle as it lies in its burrow on a sandy beach. The foot anchors the whole animal in the sand and the shells protect the soft parts. From between the shells on one side of the animal there protrude two siphons. The animal draws water in through one siphon and passes it out through the other. In this way a continuous current of water is passing through the mantle and with it go thousands of tiny plants and animals, which form part of the plankton—the floating population of the sea. These

93

particles of food are filtered off from the sea-water and trapped on the gills of the cockle. From there they are passed to the mouth. In this way cockles, mussels, oysters, razor-shells and many other animals are continually straining off their food from the sea water around them. Some of these bivalve molluscs live buried in sand, like the cockle and razor-shell, others live free on the bottom, like the scallop, while the common mussel lives attached to rocks by strong thin threads (Figure 60).

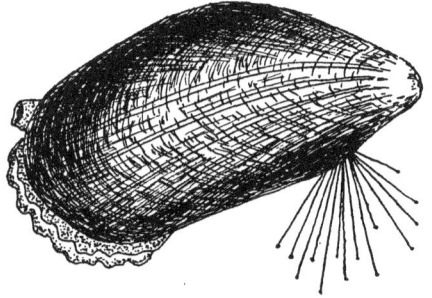

FIGURE 60

Mussel, showing the byssus threads by which it attaches itself (three-quarters natural size)

Cockles are found crowded together in sheltered sandy bays, where they are buried about one inch below the surface. There are important cockle fisheries in south Wales, on the sandy coasts of Lancashire and Cheshire, and in many other places. The cockles are harvested at low tide and sent by rail to London and other large cities. They are excellent eating and a handful of cockles in a codfish pie will turn an otherwise dull dish into something really worthwhile.

As you walk along the water's edge when the tide is out you occasionally see water spurting out of small holes in the sand. This is the razor-shell animal emptying the water through its siphons before it buries itself deeper in the sand (Figure 62). You must then dig quickly, and if you are lucky you will turn up the whole animal about a foot down in the sand.

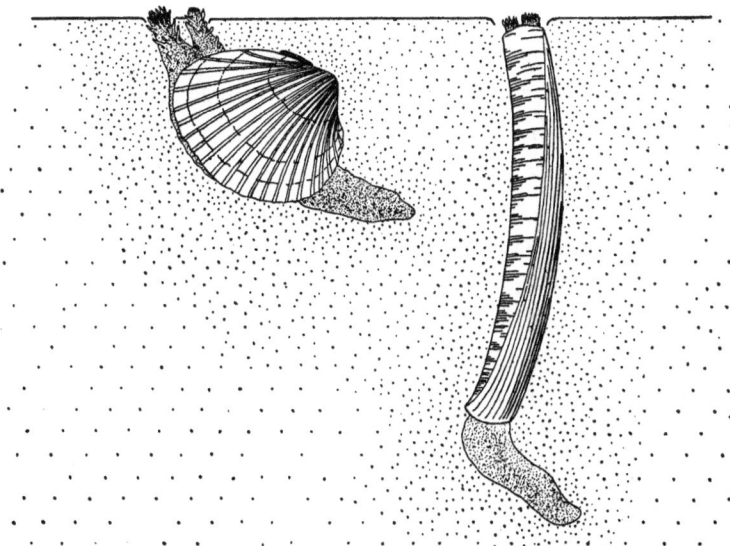

FIGURE 61   FIGURE 62

61. Cockle, drawn to show how it lies embedded in the sand, with only the two siphons appearing above the surface
62. Razor shell, drawn in the same way. The animal reaches this position by the active burrowing movements of the strong muscular foot
(one-half natural size)

The so-called ship-worm (*Teredo*) is also one of the molluscs. It has a long flabby worm-like body with very small shells at the front end. These animals do an enormous amount of damage to wooden ships and the piles of piers by burrowing into the submerged timber, eating it as they go, so that finally most of the wood has disappeared and the whole structure collapses.

Octopuses and cuttlefish are also molluscs. The shells of cuttlefishes are those flattened chalky objects—cuttle-bones—

often found washed up on the shore along the south coast, and much used by bird fanciers as a source of grit for cage birds. In the living cuttlefish this 'bone' is buried beneath the skin of the back. They feed mainly on small crabs and prawns which they catch by shooting out the two longest of their ten tentacles. Both cuttlefish and octopus are ugly animals with large eyes, but they are perhaps the most intelligent of the invertebrate animals, for they are able to learn, if only for short periods. They are, indeed, very sensitive to changes in their surroundings, and can change colour quickly when frightened or irritated. You are not likely to see them alive on the shore, but sometimes they are kept for a time in large marine aquaria. During the last few years there has been a minor plague of octopuses along the Channel coasts of England and France—a plague because the octopus enter crab pots and lobster pots and eat up the bait, and sometimes also the catch.

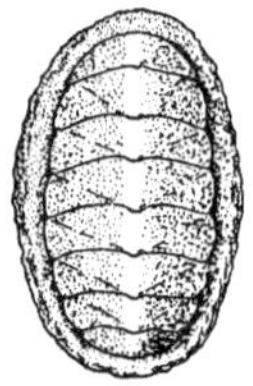

FIGURE 63

Coat-of-mail shell. This is a mollusc which clings to rocks and feeds in much the same way as a limpet, but it has a number of small shelly plates making a 'coat-of-mail', instead of a single hard shell (natural size)

The molluscs are one of the largest of all animal groups, in fact something like 70,000 different species have been described, with representatives living on land and in fresh water as well as in the sea. Many of them are very beautiful and they provide us with a food which can be one of the greatest delicacies of the table.

8. Sea Anemones, Sea-firs
and Jellyfish

As floating by or rolling on the shore,
Those living Jellies which the flesh inflame,
Fierce as a nettle, and from that its name.
Some in huge masses, some that you may bring
In the small compass of a lady's ring.

CRABBE

O N every rocky shore you will find brilliantly coloured sea anemones attached to the sides of rock pools and to the under surfaces of boulders. These are soft-bodied animals—each one a simple tube of muscle attached at one end to some firm object. At the top end of the body there is a ring of tentacles, which are used in catching food. When the tide is out these tentacles are often pulled into the body, but if you draw a finger slowly across the tentacles of an expanded sea anemone in a rock pool you will feel that they are sticky. You have, in fact, been stung by the sea anemone. For all along the tentacles there are rows of tiny sting cells which shoot out sticky threads at anything which touches them. These threads are strong enough to hold the small animals on which the sea anemone feeds, and at the same time they produce a poison which paralyses the prey.

The stings of our shore anemones are not very powerful and

H 97

they do not penetrate the skin of your finger, but there are other sea anemones and many jellyfish which can give bad stings. In some places, where there are shoals of jellyfish in summer, bathers may get a painful rash from brushing against the stinging tentacles. This does not often happen in England, but I have seen (and felt) these stinging shoals in southern Norway during the summer. In its mild form the stinging is rather like that of a bed of nettles, with quite severe sharp pain, and great irritation, but the effect varies and some people may suffer an unpleasant feeling of depression and muscle weakness lasting for twenty-four hours or more.

Jellyfish are often washed up on the shore, where they look unattractive flabby objects, but when they are alive and swimming in mid-water they are beautiful animals. They are best watched from a small boat on a clear summer day when they swim near the surface. Most jellyfish are shaped like open umbrellas, with tentacles hanging down from the edges, and a central mouth forming a handle to the umbrella (Figure 64). They swim by a kind of jet propulsion, for every time the umbrella closes it pushes out a broad jet of water and the whole jellyfish moves upwards. Then it may rest for a bit with the umbrella open, and as it does it will sink very slowly in the water, perhaps being carried sideways at the same time by the currents. A jellyfish is not the sort of animal which ever gets anywhere by its own efforts, it merely manages to keep well above the bottom and in so doing its ring of tentacles, richly supplied with sting cells, pass through much water and are able to catch small floating and swimming animals. The food caught by the tentacles is passed to the mouth and from there to the stomach which is inside the umbrella.

If you walk along the shore near high tide always keep an eye on the long ridges of dead seaweed washed up by the waves.

Sea Anemones, Sea-firs and Jellyfish

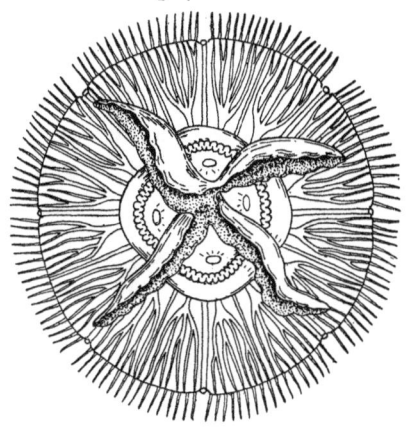

FIGURE 64

Jellyfish seen from below, showing the four arms of the handle which
join at the central mouth. The whole animal is edged by a row of
stinging tentacles (greatly reduced)

Among many other interesting things you will find the delicate
feathery tufts of sea-firs or hydroids (Figure 65) attached to the
leathery fronds of tangle-weeds. These tufts are the dead
skeletons of animals—not plants. Each branched piece is a
colony of tiny animals, each tiny animal a miniature sea
anemone. Try and find the living colonies on the tangle weeds
growing at low tide, and leave a piece in a dish of sea water so
that the tentacles can expand. The colony can be fed with the
pinhead-sized animals which you see darting about in rock
pools.

Sea anemones and sea-firs live very stationary lives, attached
to rocks and seaweeds just waiting for their food to come to
them. They are not much eaten by other animals, and certainly
not by Man. This is probably because the sting cells are un-
palatable, but in spite of this there are a few sea slugs which
browse away on sea anemone tentacles!

Sea Anemones, Sea-firs and Jellyfish

Nowadays there is a curious trade going on with the skeletons of certain kinds of sea fir. The feathery tufts are dredged from the sea bottom, mainly from shallow water near the mouth of the Thames. They are washed and dried so that the animal tissue is removed, leaving the dead horny skeletons. These

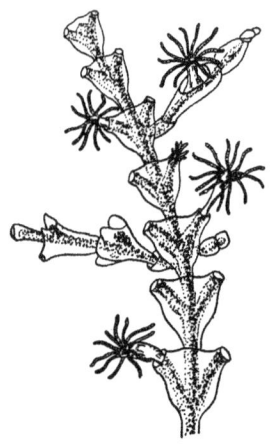

FIGURE 65

Sea fir: part of a colony greatly enlarged. Some of the animals making up the colony are expanded and show their tentacles, others are pulled back into the horny skeleton

skeletons are then dyed various colours and sold as a form of decoration under the name 'sea fern'. In Britain in recent years the value of this peculiar product has been as much as a quarter of a million pounds sterling.

On the shore the two common anemones are the beadlet and the snake-locks. The beadlet you will find on every rocky shore, and when the tide is out the tentacles are pulled back into the body. To see the real beauty of this animal you should find some which are living in rock pools where they are covered with water even at low tide. Then you can watch the elegant

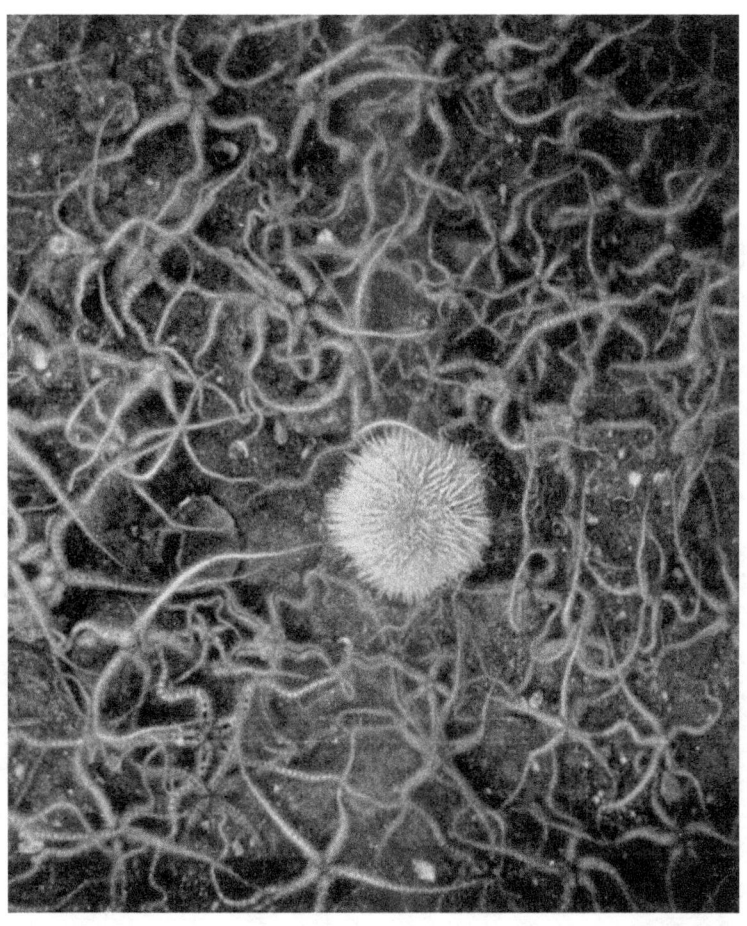

V. Photograph of the sea bottom, in a depth of 180 feet, taken with an automatic underwater camera. This picture shows a crowded mass of brittle-stars and among them a sea urchin.

(Photograph by permission of the Council of the Marine Biological Association of the United Kingdom.)

VI. Peacock fan worm, a tube dwelling worm with a magnificent ring of tentacles
(photograph, D. P. Wilson).

Sea Anemones, Sea-firs and Jellyfish

waving movements of the tentacles, and see the blue beadlets which form a ring round the base of the tentacles. In the snake-locks anemone the tentacles are much longer and they are never pulled back into the body.

Although they look as though they are permanently fixed, sea anemones can, in fact, move about very slowly, but I do not think they ever move very far. Occasionally you may find a sea anemone which is dividing into two, and when this has happened each of the half anemones produced grows quickly into a complete and separate animal.

In tropical seas great coral reefs are formed by coral polyps, another kind of sea anemone, which live in colonies and form limy skeletons round their bodies. As these corals increase in number (by division) they gradually grow upwards in the water and also spread sideways, so that a solid wall or reef of corals is formed. Of course in the process the coral animals underneath are being smothered by the newer, younger ones on top, but even the dead corals help in the formation of the reef for their skeletons are hard. In Britain we have none of these colonial corals, but we do have one or two small solitary corals, including the Devon cup coral, a most beautiful animal which lives in sheltered crevices along the coasts of Devon and Cornwall.

In a sea-water aquarium it is not difficult to keep shore anemones alive—they have often been kept successfully for many years. Although their natural food consists largely of water fleas and other small living animals they will feed quite happily on pieces of finely chopped fish or meat. If you feed them with this kind of dead food, be sure not to leave uneaten pieces lying about the floor of the tank, or they will decay and the water will become cloudy. Below low tide on rocks and piers you will find the dahlia anemone (Plate IV), well named for it looks like the flower head of a large spidery garden dahlia, as much as six inches across, and beautifully coloured. Unfortunately, these handsome animals are not really suited for small aquaria, but they live quite well in the larger public aquaria which have an efficient system of circulating and aerating the water.

If you hunt carefully among the seaweed and eelgrass at low tide you can often find the small stalked jellyfish, known as a Lucernarian (Figure 66). This is one of the treasures of the seashore, looking like an umbrella blown inside out and hanging by its handle. The tiny tentacles, sting-laden as in all the animals described in this chapter, are arranged in groups where the ribs of the umbrella meet the edge. This is an attractive animal when seen expanded in still water, but jog the dish in which you are keeping it, and it will quickly contract into a shapeless mass of jelly.

Sea-firs and sea anemones can be seen on all our shores, but more especially on rocky stretches where they can find a firm anchorage. They are among the most characteristic and beautiful of all sea animals, and with care it is not difficult to keep them alive and watch their interesting method of feeding.

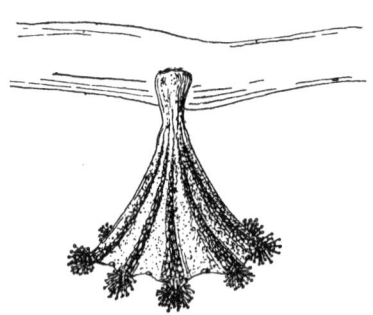

FIGURE 66

A lucernarian, related to the jellyfish. They live, attached to seaweed and eelgrass, near low water mark (natural size)

9. Sea Urchins, Starfishes and Sea Cucumbers

As there are stars in the sky, so are there stars in the sea.
J. H. LINCK in *De stellis marinis* (1733), the
first book published on starfishes

THE common starfish can be found at low water sheltering behind boulders and in rock pools. It has five arms (Figure 67) and when held in the hand it feels rough, especially on the upper surface; this is because there are hundreds of short spines in the skin. These spines are not really sharp, nor are they poisonous; in the past few years I have handled over 6,000 of these starfish and have never suffered from any rash or skin poisoning. But starfishes can be a serious pest in beds oʟ oysters and mussels, for they eat these molluscs greedily. If you turn a starfish over, so that it lies on its upper surface you will see that there is a groove along the undersurface of each arm; these grooves meet in the centre at the mouth. In the arm grooves there are hundreds of soft, waving semi-transparent tube-feet. The tube-feet are filled with a watery liquid and are all connected with each other by water channels which run along each arm and round the central disc. The tiny discs at the ends of the tube-feet can attach themselves very firmly to stones and rocks, and by hauling on its attached tube-feet the starfish is able to move about. Sometimes if you pull a starfish quickly off a rock it will leave behind a number of these tube-feet discs. The tube-feet are also used by the starfish in opening the shells

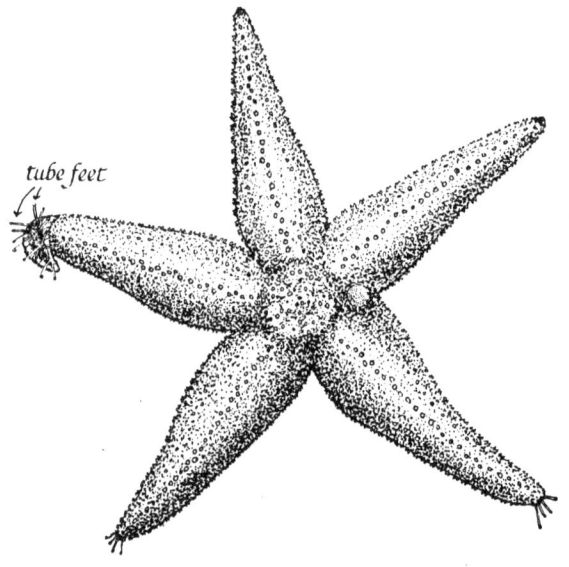

tube feet

FIGURE 67

Common starfish, from above. Two of the arms are turned back at the tips and show a few tube-feet (one-half natural size)

of oysters, mussels and similar molluscs. To do this the starfish fixes its arms astride the shells of a mussel, usually with two arms on one shell and three on the other; the fixing of the arms is done entirely by the tube-feet. The starfish then starts to pull on the two shells of the mussel. At first nothing happens, for the mussel can hold its shells closed for quite a time, but eventually the mussel becomes tired and the starfish is then able to pull the shells apart. As soon as the mussel shells begin to gape the star-fish turns its own stomach more or less inside out. In this way it comes in contact with the mussel flesh which it softens with the juices from its stomach and then digests. I have watched starfishes feeding on mussels and scallops in aquarium tanks and have found that they usually take two to three hours to open the shells. Starfish are the only animals which feed in exactly this way. On an oyster bed each starfish may eat four to five oysters a week, and each of these oysters has probably taken two to three years to reach a reasonable size, so that a few hundred starfishes can cause considerable losses to an oyster grower.

At one time oystermen used to dredge up starfishes, tear them apart, and then throw the pieces overboard again. But this was not a very good method of reducing the numbers of starfish, because each piece, provided it had a section of the central disc attached, could then start to grow and would eventually have formed a complete starfish. This power of regeneration is very common among starfishes, and on the shore you will often find starfishes with an arm or two missing, and the beginnings of the new arms just appearing.

The Gibbous starlet (Figure 68) is a much smaller starfish, commonly found under rocks when the tide is out, and usually only about 1¼ inches across. It lives rather well in small aquaria.

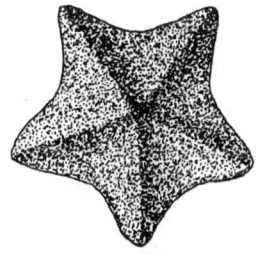

FIGURE 68

Gibbous starlet; a small starfish found on some rocky shores (three-quarters natural size)

Sea Urchins, Starfishes and Sea Cucumbers

Rather like the common starfish are the brittle-stars which have five very flexible jointed arms, thickly set with thin spines, but they do not have the leathery skin of the starfish and are usually much smaller. The spines are not poisonous. The larger brittle-stars are about four inches across the arms, but starfishes reach much larger sizes; the biggest I have ever handled was a common starfish twenty-four inches across the arms; this was not from the shore, but was trawled up in deeper water. If you search carefully among the tufts of red coralline seaweed growing in rock pools you can often find a small brittle-star not more than one inch across. These animals do not feed like starfishes, but rely for most of their food on small pieces of dead and dying animals and plants. In fact out at sea they act as scavengers, feeding on odd scraps of food on the bottom, and on the dead plankton animals and plants which rain down from above. In Plate V you will see a photograph of an area of sea bottom, twenty inches by twenty inches, about six miles south of Looe in Cornwall. This picture was taken with an automatic camera working in a depth of 200 feet, and it shows a very crowded mass of brittle-stars as they appear on the bottom. This photograph shows between twenty and thirty brittle-stars and they were as dense as this over a very large area.

The underwater photograph (Plate V) also shows a sea urchin lying on the bottom among the brittle-stars. Sea urchins of this type can be found on the shore, or, at any rate, just below low water. They have a hard, brittle shell covered with long spines. The Greek scientist Aristotle made some very accurate observations on sea urchins which are common in the Mediterranean, where they are used as food. He wrote: 'singularly enough, the urchin has what we may call its head and its mouth down below, and a place for the issue of the residuum up above. For the food on which the creature lives lies down below; consequently the mouth has a position well adapted for getting at the food.' Inside the mouth there is a set of five jaws worked by a complex mechanical system of plates and muscles. This apparatus was also described by Aristotle, and indeed it is now known as Aristotle's lantern.

On the movement of the sea urchin Aristotle wrote: 'The urchin uses its spines as feet, for it rests its weight on these, and then moving shifts from place to place', and to a certain extent this is accurate. It might be better to say that the sea urchin pulls itself along the surface of the rocks by means of its spines and tube-feet. It feeds on the small weeds and barnacles encrusting the rocks, which it scrapes off with the jaws of the lantern. The large sea urchin is four to five inches across, and these are common near the shore in Scotland, usually attached to rocks, and I have often seen them crawling on wooden piers in the lochs on the west coast of Scotland. Along the south coast of England they do not usually appear on the shore, but they are common in deeper water. Instead you will often find on the shore a smaller sea urchin, not more than two inches across, and with a more flattened shell. On sandy shores you can dig up the little heart-urchin, which, as the name implies is heart-shaped instead of being round. The heart-urchin is dull yellowish in colour, and it makes a burrow in the sand five to seven inches deep. There it feeds, not as was once thought by just shovelling sand into its mouth like an earthworm but by picking up little morsels of food (mostly dead plant and animal remains) with its tube-feet and passing them to the mouth.

Occasionally on the shore, if you are hunting carefully under stones you may find a whitish sausage-shaped animal with a ring of tentacles at one end. This is a sea cucumber (Figure 69), another animal which has tube-feet arranged in five rows along its body. Sea cucumbers feed by using their sticky tentacles to gather food particles from the mud. When the tentacles are loaded they are drawn into the mouth and the particles are literally licked off. Sea cucumbers are, in fact, scavengers, eaters of the debris which gathers on the sea floor, and which consists mainly of broken up pieces of dead plants and animals.

Sea urchins, starfishes, brittle-stars, and sea cucumbers are grouped together under the name 'echinoderms', which merely means the 'spiny-skinned ones'. They are really quite unlike any of the other animals which you meet on the shore or on land, for no other living things have this elaborate hydraulic system working soft flexible tube-feet. I have always found that they are among the most interesting of all sea animals, partly on account of this peculiar method of moving and feeding, but also because of the different ways in which they use limy plates and spines for protection. If you take a dead sea urchin, one of the round ones is best, and carefully rub off the spines, you will be left with the shell, which is made up of radiating rows of cleverly arranged interlocking plates. All these plates have been formed by the skin of the sea urchin, and have in fact been part of its living body. Some of the plates are pierced by tiny holes, and it was through these holes that the tube-feet appeared when the sea urchin was alive. You can also notice that these pierced plates are arranged in five of the rays of the shells and that in between the tube-feet rays there are rows of plates which are not pierced by holes. The domed shell of the sea urchin must, indeed, have been the envy of many an architect, for it would be difficult to build on land such a fine shape with so little material, and certainly you are unlikely to find anything more beautifully constructed on the seashore.

Common starfishes are usually red-brown in colour, but you find them pale pink, or brick-red or even violet. In the sea urchins the colours of the shell and spines are more usually purple, while the 'cotton-spinner', a large sea cucumber which lives offshore, is coloured orange and black. This wide range of bright colours is another of the great attractions of this group of animals, which makes the study of them so interesting.

In general, though, the starfishes, sea urchins and sea cucumbers are of no real use to Man. It is true one can eat and enjoy the roe of some sea urchins, and that in the east the Chinese make a good soup from certain kinds of sea cucumbers, but these uses are more than balanced by the serious damage which starfishes can do to shellfish beds.

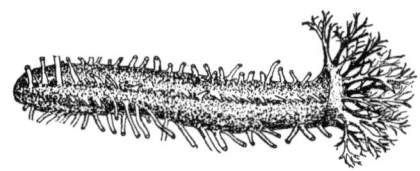

FIGURE 69

Sea cucumber (two-thirds natural size)

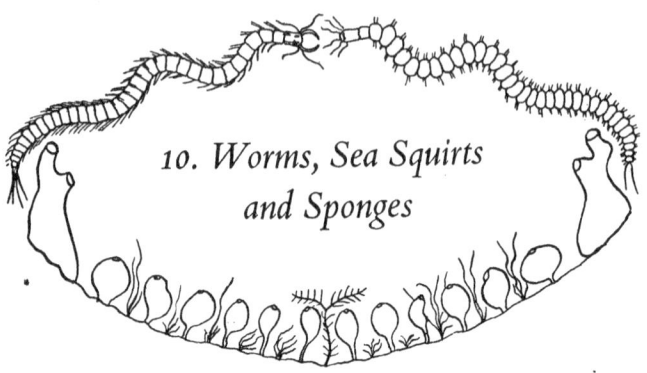

10. Worms, Sea Squirts and Sponges

The sponge breeds parasites, worms, and other creatures, on which, if they be detached, the rock-fishes prey, as they prey also on the remaining stumps of the sponge; but, if the sponge be broken off, it grows again from the remaining stump and the place is soon as well covered as before.

ARISTOTLE, *Historia Animalium*
(D'Arcy Thompson's translation)

THERE are many different kinds of worms on the seashore as well as in the open sea. Some of them live on the bottom among stones and rocks and under seaweeds, and others live actually buried in the sand or mud. On sandy shores you will often find a worm known as the sand mason because of the beautifully constructed tube of sand grains in which it lives (Figure 70). An inch or two of this tube sticks up above the surface of the sand, and without this you would never find it. Another tube-builder is the peacock fan worm (Plate VI) which lives near low-water mark on muddy shores and makes a tube of mud mixed with slime. It has a fine ring of delicate tentacles round the mouth and these protrude from the top end of the tube when the tide is in and the shore is covered with water. Peacock fan worms are not difficult to keep in an aquarium and they are very beautiful when the tentacles are expanded.

Worms, Sea Squirts and Sponges

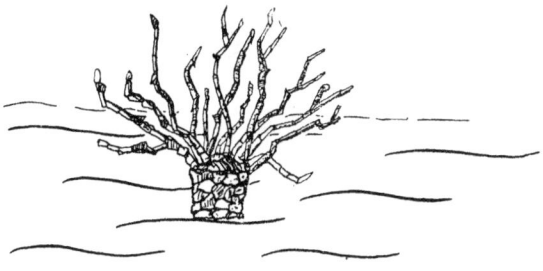

FIGURE 70

Sand mason worm. This drawing shows the crown of the tube which sticks up above the surface of the sand. The tube is made by the worm itself (natural size)

Lugworms, which are so much used as bait by sea anglers, are also tube dwellers. They live in U-shaped tunnels in the sand, and keep the walls of the tunnels from collapsing by coating them with a slimy secretion. They can burrow to a depth of two feet and are particularly common in muddy sand, and in and around cockle beds. Lugworms feed by eating the sand in which they live. Inside their bodies they digest the small particles of food which are nearly always present, and the remainder is then passed out of their bodies in the form of sand casts, which are so common on bathing beaches.

On rocky shores ragworms (Figure 71) are found hidden under stones and among seaweeds, especially in the tufts of red *Corallina* weed which fringe the rock pools. These worms are eaten by crabs and fishes, and they make a good bait for certain kinds of fish. They swim by a wriggling wave movement of the whole body. At the front end of a ragworm, if you can get one which is not wriggling, you will see two sharp jaws, each shaped like an elephant tusk; these jaws are used to seize the small animals and pieces of dead animal on which they feed. On rocky

Worms, Sea Squirts and Sponges

FIGURE 71

Ragworm (natural size)

shores there are many other free-living worms, which hunt for food like the ragworms, but there are other worms which sit still and wait for food to come to them; some of these live in limy tubes attached to rocks and seaweeds. These tubes, like the sand tube of the sand mason, are all built by the worms themselves. One of the commonest is the Spirorbis worm (Figure 72) which lives in small coiled tubes cemented to rocks or to the fronds of the larger brown seaweeds. When the tide is out, and that is when you are most likely to find these tubes, there will be no sign of the worms themselves, for they will all have withdrawn into their tubes. But if you take a piece of seaweed with a tube on it, and place it in a glass of sea water the worm will soon protrude

Worms, Sea Squirts and Sponges

FIGURE 72

Spirobis worm. A tube-worm which settles on a rock or a piece of seaweed and makes its own shelly tube. The drawing shows the tentacles of the worm coming out of the mouth of the tube (greatly enlarged)

its head end which is surrounded by a ring of tentacles, rather like those of the peacock fan worm, but much smaller. This happened when the swimming crab in Figure 45 was being drawn, and in the back right hand corner of its shell you will see the small limy tube of the worm which had settled there. The next time the crab moulted its shell would be cast away and with it the little tube-worm, which from then on would feed in one place only, instead of being carried around by the crab.

Quite different from the worms are the sea squirts, a group of animals which occur only in the sea. You can find sea squirts on the shore between tides, but to find one quickly it is best to row alongside a pier at low tide. Just below the water surface, attached to the pier, you should see a number of transparent jelly-like sacs; these will be sea squirts (Figure 73). If the light is behind them you will be able to see right through them, and you will notice that there are openings at the free end. These openings are comparable with the siphons of a cockle, for water enters the body at one of them and leaves by the other. The ingoing stream of sea water carries with it food in the form of

I   113

plankton and particles of dead matter, and in the body of the sea squirt this is filtered out of the water and passed into the stomach. If you squeeze one of these animals you will understand why they are called sea squirts.

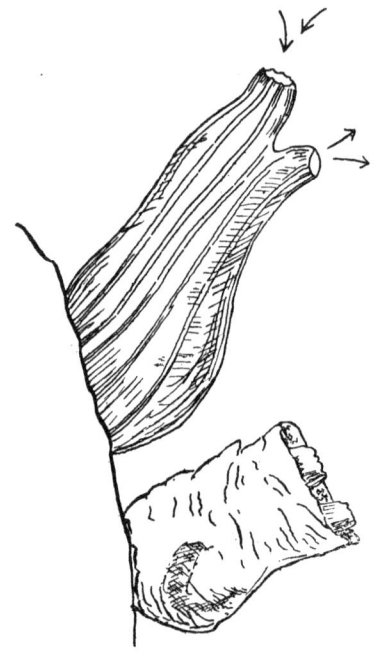

FIGURE 73

Sea squirts. The upper one expanded, the lower one contracted. The arrows show the direction of the water currents which carry food to the animal (natural size)

The sea squirt is yet another animal which feeds by straining plankton out of the sea water. It is difficult at first to realize the extent to which quite large marine animals rely for their food on very small or even microscopic particles. The filter feeding of mussels and cockles, the mud gathering of the sea cucumbers,

114

and the sand gobbling of lugworms and many other tube-worms show how varied may be the methods of dealing with these tiny particles.

The sponges also feed by taking their food from the sea in the form of small particles; some sponges are very common on the seashore in Britain, where they are usually quite small. Bath sponges and Turkish cup sponges, which grow to a large size, are only found in the warmer water of the tropics and sub-tropics. The undersides of large rocks at low tide are often festooned with purse sponges, each a colony of animals growing in the shape of a flattened purse, one to three inches long. They are attached at one end to the rock, while the other end hangs free in the water. When the tide is in, sea water is swept through the wall of the sponge by millions of microscopic hair-like cilia. As this water passes through, the food particles in it are extracted by the cells of the sponge and digested. The filtered water which has thus entered the central cavity of the purse is then passed out through the large hole at the free end of the sponge. These large holes can be seen very clearly in the ordinary bath sponge. Another shore sponge which is very common on the shore, is the bread crumb sponge, which grows in irregular soft masses encrusting the undersides of boulders. Sometimes pieces of this sponge break free in a storm and they are often found washed up at high water mark, and you can distinguish them from other animal remains by the holes which perforate the crust of the sponge at intervals.

Offshore in deeper water there are even more kinds of sponges, many of which are branched like small bushes, and coloured yellow, orange and red. On the shore the smaller encrusting sponges which grow round the sides of rock pools make a beautiful vividly coloured carpet-like background for the more active animals which may be stranded there between tides.

11. Rocky Shores and Sandy Shores

Or, in their pearly shells at ease, attend
Moist nutriment; or under rocks their food
In jointed armour watch. . . .
                                        MILTON

WE have already seen some of the difficulties under which animals and plants must live on a rocky shore. Briefly these are the battering by the waves, the scouring action of the tides, drenching by fresh water in rainy weather, and exposure to the heat and drying action of the sun at low tide. The fact that so many living things do survive on the seashore shows how successful they have been in adapting themselves to these varying hazards.

On the sides and upper surfaces of the rocks and large boulders there are heavy growths of seaweeds, mostly wracks. On some rocks acorn barnacles may also occupy large areas, in fact it seems as though wracks and barnacles do actually compete for space. The streamlined shape of the barnacles is well fitted to stand up to the heavy battering of waves. By shutting the valves at the top of their limy boxes barnacles can close themselves up in a self-contained tent, and at the same time they enclose a bubble of air. On a quiet day when the tide is out you can hear

VII. An oiled gannet at the foot of the cliffs on Ailsa Craig, Firth of Clyde. The black oil has covered the upper part of the white breast plumage.

VIII. A pilot whale hunt in the Faeroe Islands. The boats are driving the whales on shore, where they will be killed and used for food.

Rocky Shores and Sandy Shores

the 'tut-tut' sound of thousands of acorn barnacles closing the valves of the shells tighter as they feel the vibration of your feet on the rocks.

Limpets, too, manage to survive on the top of exposed rocks, but most other animals, such as winkles, top-shells, and dog whelks, crawl to the sides of the rocks where there is some shelter from the sun. If you are hunting for the common edible periwinkle you will often find them lined up in rows in the cracks between rocks, or hidden away singly under the dangling fronds of toothed wrack.

The zoning of the animals and seaweeds on the shore is always interesting. The seaweeds change from channelled wrack at high tide to toothed wrack just above low water with bladder wrack and knotted wrack in between, and the large tangle-weeds grow only around low-water mark and in deeper water. The different kinds of winkles are also found living at different levels on the shore, and there are other examples of this zoning. In the middle levels of the shore among the knotted wrack you will find the top-shells most common, but above them the brown, white, yellow or striped shells of the dog whelk will be more obvious. There is, however, no hard and fast boundary between the zones of animals, and on some rocky shores you will see a great mixing of the zones.

Another interesting place to hunt for seashore animals is beneath the stones that litter most rocky beaches, especially beneath those stones which can easily be turned over. There a number of animals shelter while the tide is out. I have already mentioned the presence in these places of worm pipe-fishes and Cornish suckers which apparently do not mind being left almost dry for some hours. With them you will find ragworms sometimes as much as five inches in length which will wriggle away as soon as they are exposed to the light. There will also be common

Rocky Shores and Sandy Shores

shore crabs, and nearly always those little sideways flattened sandhopper shrimps which slip from your fingers as though they had been greased and scuffle away in the muddy sand. If you do look for animals living under stones, be sure and replace the stones when you have finished. Great destruction can occur when the stones are left bottom side up, for if the sun is shining the animals will probably be dried up, and whatever the weather the seagulls will quickly eat up any small fishes and crabs which are exposed in this way.

It is on the lower reaches of the shore just above and below low-tide mark that you find such large numbers of different animals, and the lower the tide falls the more chance you have of seeing them. That is why for shore collecting you should always choose the time of spring tides (at new moon or full moon) when the tide falls so much lower on the shore than at other times. Then you will find sea squirts and sponges attached to the undersides of rocks, or living on the edges of rock pools. In small rock crevices there are often specimens of the dirty-white sea cucumber, while nearby, where there is more room, you may see a purple-spined sea urchin wedged into a sheltered corner and held in place by its spines and tube-feet.

On a sandy shore the animals are often present in large numbers, and yet you hardly ever see them. In fact unless you dig, and dig fast, you will not find a sandy shore so interesting. If only you could watch the surface of the sand in a sheltered bay when the tide is in you would see things coming to life. Shrimps would dart around feeding on odd scraps, and an occasional weever fish would swim past. The siphons of cockles and razor-shells would appear above the surface of the sand, and at almost regular intervals the 'sand casts' of the lugworm would grow in size as more and more waste sand is expelled by the worm living in its U-shaped tube. At low tide all you may see are these sand casts and the regular rows of sand ripples which can be so tiring to walk over. Perhaps a hundred yards ahead there is a flock of waders, strung along the water's edge, and this is a sign that the sand is not as dull and empty as it may appear. For these waders will be feeding on worms and small crustaceans of types which live buried in the sand, living in fact in the water which fills in the spaces between the sand grains.

Nowadays the sand can be watched when the tide is in by using a self-contained diving suit, or even just a breathing tube which allows you to breathe while you are a few feet under water. Or you can watch the sand in comfort from a small rowing boat. If you do this you will often find that the ripples of the sea make it almost impossible to see the sand. You can get over this difficulty by using a glass-bottomed box. The joins where the glass meets the wood must be water-tight but otherwise the box need not be elaborate. The top of the box is left open. By resting the box, glass downwards, on the surface of the water you smooth out the ripples, and you will then be able to see the bottom quite clearly, provided the depth of water is not too great.

One may well ask what all these animals are doing on the shore, how they are living and feeding. Gradually by studying them on the shore or in aquarium tanks people have got to know quite a bit about their feeding habits and way of life. A good way of gathering all this information together is in the form of a food chain, which tells you what eats what. Figure 74 is an attempt at giving some of the links in the food chain on a rocky shoreline broken up by little sandy bays. If you start at the plankton, which are the very small animals and plants floating in the sea, and follow the arrows, you will see that the plankton is eaten by many very different animals, among them mussels, oysters, cockles, sea squirts and barnacles. As we have already

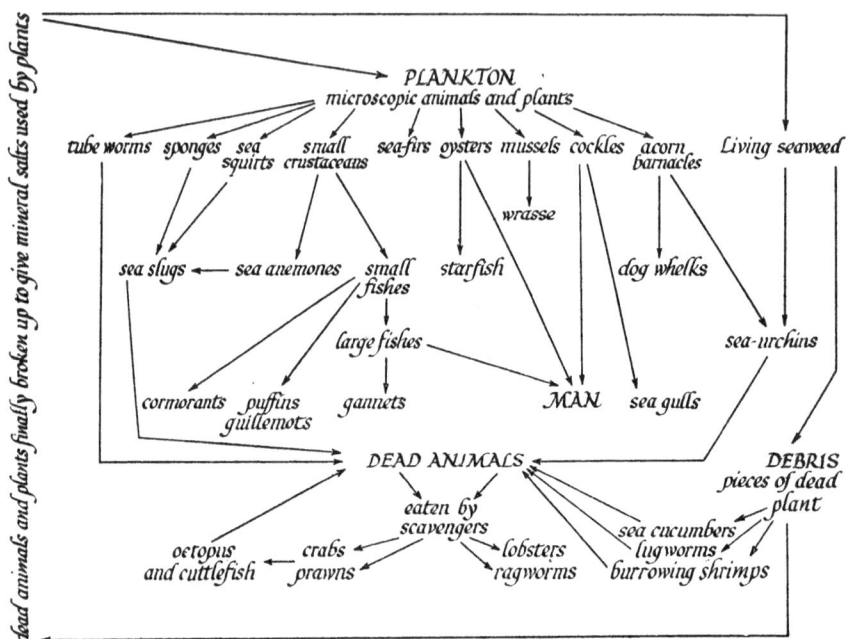

FIGURE 74

Food chain on a rocky shore. This diagram shows what eats what.
Start at 'Plankton' and follow the arrows, for example, plankton
is eaten by small crustaceans which are eaten by sea anemones and
small fishes. The latter are eaten by larger fishes which are in turn
eaten by Man and gannets. There are, of course, hundreds of other
links but those shown are some of the more important ones

seen, all these animals have some method of straining the
plankton from the water. These plankton-feeders are in
their turn eaten by other animals—starfishes, dog whelks and
small fishes, which are then eaten by large fishes, birds or by
Man. Equally interesting are the side chains showing the part
played by debris eaters, scavengers, and the larger seaweeds.
But this chart is by no means complete, and there are many

other links which could be put in, and also many links of which we have no knowledge.

In a rock pool on the shore you can study a little self-contained world, full of interesting animals and plants all quite cut off from the outside world when the tide is out. I once found a rock pool about nine feet by six feet in surface area, where the main links in the food chain were those given in Figure 75. This arrangement would probably not last long, because at the next tide a

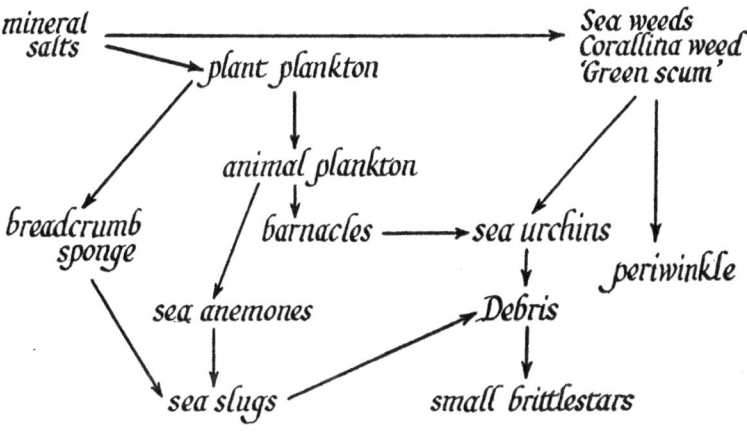

FIGURE 75

Food chain in a rock pool. The same kind of links as in Figure 74, but fewer and less complicated

small lobster or crab, or a father lasher might get stranded in the pool, and then all the links would be upset and the food chain would look quite different. In fact you will find that no groups of living animals and plants remain the same for long. There is always some change and development going on, and this is especially true on the seashore.

12. Driftline Treasures and Tragedies

There is a pleasure in the pathless woods,
There is a rapture on the lonely shore,
There is society where none intrudes,
By the deep sea, and music in its roar.

BYRON

A walk along the drift line near high-water mark is interesting not only for the enormous hordes of sandhoppers, flies and other animals which live in the warm sticky heaps of decaying seaweed but also because of many other interesting things cast up by the tide. Much of this consists of the remains of animals—the cast skeletons of crabs, shells of sea urchins, cuttlebones, and empty egg cases of dogfish, ray and whelk. It is the unexpected finds which can be so interesting—the water-worn bottle glass, the corks and floats from fishermen's nets, dead animals from other parts of the Atlantic Ocean, amber from the Baltic, and the lengths of sea-rubbed timber with a satisfying soft worn surface. Perhaps the wood has come from the forests of northern Europe, or possibly only from a wooded creek ten miles down channel.

It is always of interest to know the origin of the more unusual items of shore drift. Along the east coast of England and Scot-

Driftline Treasures and Tragedies

land there is certainly a possibility that some of the oddments have come from the far north. On the western shores of Britain and especially in south-western England there is usually no doubt at all. Queer, out of the ordinary, creatures, often dead, are washed up on the shore, and they have almost certainly come from the seas to the south-west, carried in to our shores by the slow-moving warm water from the region of the West Indies and the Gulf of Mexico. Every now and again turtles are found on shores in England. During the first eighteen days of December 1938 no fewer than seven of these reptiles were stranded on the coasts of Britain. Four of these were loggerhead turtles, of which two came ashore at Bognor, one on Selsey Bill, and one at Tenby in south Wales. Normally such turtles would die fairly soon, because the water around our coasts is too cold for them, but a few years ago a small turtle found in Cornwall was brought into the Plymouth aquarium and lived there for some weeks.

Lengths of timber washed up on the shore are always worth a careful examination. If the timber has been in the water for any length of time it is almost certain to have been bored by some marine animal. The most destructive of these boring animals is *Teredo*, often known as the ship-worm although it is not really a worm (discussed on p. 95). *Teredo* is, in fact, a bivalve mollusc, like the cockle and mussel, but it has become peculiarly adapted to a life of burrowing into timber. After a free-swimming stage in the plankton the young *Teredo* settles down on a piece of wood, and using the shells as raspers it proceeds to burrow its way in. Once it is inside it turns and bores along the grain of the wood, and makes a long burrow, often some feet in length and about half an inch in diameter. The worm-like part of *Teredo* is made up of the two very long siphons fused together, and they secrete a shelly case which lines the walls of the burrow. At one

Driftline Treasures and Tragedies

time when ships were made of wood the attacks of the ship-worm were a constant menace. Nowadays ships are either all metal, or if made of wood they can have their hulls sheathed in copper, and so the ship-worm is no longer a serious problem to ship-owners. It still does a great deal of damage to fixed wooden structures in the sea and in particular to piers and jetties.

There are other borers of timber which you may also find in a piece of driftline timber. Of these the most common is the gribble, a small crustacean, looking like a wood-louse but less than a quarter of an inch long. The gribble gnaws away at the timber with its jaws, quite often attacking the wood between the ship-worm's burrows.

Pieces of timber may also hold a colony of goose barnacles, which we have already discussed in the chapter on crustaceans. These are attractive animals even out of water, but are more interesting if you can get them into a dish of water and watch them scoop-netting for plankton with their feathery feet. In the south-west of England you may come across a group of goose barnacles which are not attached to a piece of timber or other floating object. This will probably be the buoy-making barnacle. As the name implies this barnacle makes its own gas-filled buoy, which keeps it afloat.

There are other marine animals which produce a bubble or a bladder of air, and with its help are able to float without effort on the surface of the sea. One of these is the Portuguese Man o' War, zoologically a relation of the sea-firs and jellyfish, which consists of a large inflated air bladder supporting a crowded colony of polyps, each with tentacles studded with vicious sting cells. The stings of these cells produce a most serious rash on the skin, which may be lethal, so it is just as well that they are rare here, and only seen when brought in to our shores by a series of south-westerly gales. Another drifting colony belonging to the same group is the 'by-the-wind sailor', which floats by means of many small gas bubbles in its tissues. It also has a sail cleverly set at an angle to the long axis of the body so that it catches the wind and is blown along like a little boat. It captures morsels of plankton by the long rows of tentacles, again richly supplied with sting cells, which hang down into the water below it. The by-the-wind sailor is one of the most attractive of driftline treasures, being bright blue with a silvery sail with iridescent reflections, but all the same I would avoid the tentacles and only pick it up by the sail which has no sting cells and is quite harmless.

We read a lot in the papers nowadays about the presence of oil on some of our holiday beaches. This is a problem which has only arisen during this century as ships have become more and more dependent upon various types of fuel oil. All too often ships clear out their waste oil at sea, where it floats and spreads out into a thin film, persisting for a long time. These sheets of oil are blown along the surface of the sea by the prevailing winds, and are finally washed ashore. where they form oily tidemarks. Sometimes the oil on the shore is almost liquid but in many places I have found it in solid lumps about as hard as plasticine. Whichever form it is in there is no doubt that it is very unpleasant to meet a patch of it when one is walking along the shore, for shoes and clothes can soon become caked with it. We can, at least, avoid the oil and complain about it. This the sea birds cannot do, and every year thousands of them die after their feathers have become clogged with oil. It is mainly guillemots, razorbills, puffins and gannets which suffer in this way, for they are birds which not only have to dive through the surface layer of the sea in order to catch their food, but which also spend much time swimming about on the surface (Plate VII).

Whether they are diving or swimming sea birds can scarcely

avoid the oil which quickly forms a slimy film on the breast feathers and on the wings. When the feathers are clogged the birds can no longer fly as the oiled wings are incapable of lifting the body from the water. This is bad enough, but I have always believed that the main cause of death in oiled birds is cold. For in normal healthy birds the feathers of the body, including the down feathers, act in the same way as a couple of woollen jerseys do for us. When the feathers are covered with oil they lose all their feathery properties and are no longer able to hold the layer of air which is really responsible for insulating the warm body from the cold outside. If the oiled birds no longer have a good insulating plumage, water will get in and soak the skin and there is nothing they can do to prevent this, for a bird has no way of cleaning itself of such a thick sticky oil. It is possible for a skilled person to clean the oil from sea birds, but it takes a long time. On occasions a few bird lives may be saved in this way, but it only touches the fringe of the problem.

To get some idea of the number of birds affected I once made a count of oiled birds along a stretch of shore on Ailsa Craig in the Firth of Clyde, and found that there was one bird oiled every two to three yards of coastline. This was a particularly bad bout of oiling but smaller numbers of these wretched birds are often seen along the shore.

It has been thought that if the ships cleaned out their waste oil a good distance from land, say 100 miles out, then the oil would have a chance to break up and disappear before it reached the shore. It is by no means certain that this will happen. Efforts are being made to find out the route taken by such floating oil as it drifts in from the Atlantic Ocean. It is known that the main movement of water in our part of the Atlantic is from south-west to north-east, but less is known about the detailed movements of water and oil on the surface. As an aid to tracking the

Driftline Treasures and Tragedies

path of these surface currents oceanographers make use of drift bottles. These are like small lemonade bottles, and when thrown out from ships at sea they float at the surface and are carried along by the currents. Some of them will eventually be washed ashore in Britain, France, Norway or elsewhere. The person who finds the bottle will find a note inside giving the serial number of the bottle and asking him to report the time and place of recovery. The note also promises a small reward for sending in this report.

By plotting on a chart the position at which each bottle was put into the sea and where it was later found, one gets a good idea of the direction of the surface currents. From the time taken for the bottle's drift to the shore we may also learn something of the speed of the current. It is quite possible that you may find one of these bottles during a walk along the shore. The latest idea is to use plastic envelopes instead of glass bottles. These envelopes will be dropped far out in the Atlantic by aircraft of R.A.F. Coastal Command, and in time some of them should be recovered on our shores.

Just as the drift-bottle method helps to track the movements of the surface waters of the sea, so the ringing of birds is used as a means of tracing their migrations. Birds are ringed with a metal band attached round the leg. The band bears a number and an address to which the ring should be sent if it is ever recovered —in Britain the rings should go to the British Museum (Natural History) in London. Birds may be ringed as chicks while they are still on the nest, or as adults which are caught in special traps, and released after the ring has been attached.

The driftline often yields dead birds, and it is always worth-while to check whether one of their legs bears a ring. A kitti-wake ringed on its nest on Lundy Island, Devon in July 1950 was recovered in Newfoundland in May 1951, and an Arctic

Driftline Treasures and Tragedies

Tern ringed in Ayrshire in June 1951 was found at Durban in South Africa in November of the same year. These are by no means isolated cases, and the careful collection of ringing recoveries over a number of years has given much information on bird movements.

The story of the driftline strandings is the story of many small incidents, some relating to the neighbouring shore but some related only to storm and gales which have whipped up waves thousands of miles away. These waves have travelled the Atlantic for days and weeks collecting and delivering the numerous and varied objects which make the driftline one of the most exciting parts of our seashore.

13. The Sea Beyond the Shore

To speak the truth, our own seas have been almost as little explored, although they teem with curious and unknown animals.

JOHN VAUGHAN THOMPSON in *Zoological Researches* (1830)

THE floor of the sea slopes away gradually beyond low tide, and off the mouth of the English Channel it reaches a depth of 100 fathoms (600 feet) at a distance of about 80 to 100 miles from Land's End in Cornwall. This area of sea bottom between low water and the 100-fathom line is the Continental Shelf—and it is really an underwater continuation of the continents and larger islands. Beyond the shelf, to the north and west of Britain, the sea bottom runs away more steeply, so that the depth increases quickly. This zone is the Continental Slope, which extends from the 100-fathom line to depths of about 1½ miles, beyond which you get to the really deep water, where there are depths of two to four miles or more. The greatest depths recorded are in the Pacific Ocean, where there have been soundings of over five miles. In fact some of these large holes are deeper by some 3,000 feet than the height of Mount Everest.

It is the Continental Shelf area which is the most interesting to us, as it contains all the great fishing grounds of the world. In

The Sea Beyond the Shore

European and Arctic waters nearly all commercial fishing for bottom-living fishes is done by steam or diesel-driven trawlers fitted with the otter trawl, although some fishing boats still use long lines with baited hooks for catching cod.

The otter trawl (Figure 76) is a net in the form of a bag with a large opening at the front end, tapering to a narrow 'cod-end' at the back. The trawl is drawn along the bottom by two steel

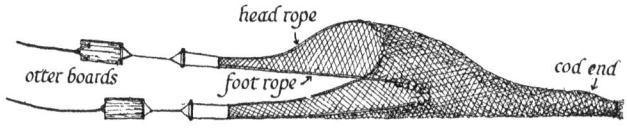

FIGURE 76

Otter trawl, seen from the side, as it fishes along the sea bottom

ropes controlled from the trawler. The mouth of the trawl is not kept open by any kind of rigid frame, but near the point where the ropes join the net there are two stout wooden otter boards. These boards are attached in such a way that they act as kites and move outwards when the trawler pulls on the ropes, and so keep the mouth of the net spread. The head rope of the trawl is kept up off the ground by a series of floats. With this kind of trawl great quantities of cod, haddock, plaice, halibut, hake and many other fishes are caught—all being fish which feed on the sea bottom. The trawl also brings in scallops, lobsters and crabs, as well as large amounts of what the fishermen call trawl rubbish—clumps of sea-fir, bright red starfishes, purple-spined sea urchins, empty shells, small crabs and sea anemones. These animals of the trawl rubbish are of no value to the fishermen and they are shovelled overboard as soon as possible. Amongst them there are animals of great interest,

The Sea Beyond the Shore

some of them similar to those found on the seashore but with more variety of species and a greater range of colour.

The long-distance trawlers working out of Grimsby, Hull, Milford Haven and Aberdeen catch their fish round Iceland and the Faeroe Islands, off Western Scotland, Western Greenland and in the White Sea to the north-east of Norway. Most of the catch in these areas is cod, with smaller quantities of halibut, hake and other fishes. In the North Sea the short-distance trawlers fish for a more varied catch, of which a high proportion may be plaice and sole, which fetch a good price on the market. It is difficult to realize the scale of trawler fishing without a visit to one of the larger fishing ports. To watch the landing and marketing of a trawler's catch at Grimsby or Hull is a most striking experience. It is not uncommon for a distant water trawler to sell its catch after a three-week trip for £5,000 to £6,000. This money is by no means all profit. The expenses of one of these trawling trips are very high, for they include not only fuel for the ship and wages for the crew, but a big outlay of money on the trawl and otter boards, and on ice to keep the fish fresh during the long voyage home. If the trawl catches on a rock, or on an uncharted piece of wreckage it may be torn, or in some cases the whole net may be lost, and this involves the trawler owners in additional expense.

There are also fisheries for those fishes which live and feed in mid-water, instead of on the sea bottom. In Europe the most important of these is the herring which is caught by drifters. In drift-netting the fishermen set out long lengths of netting in the form of a wall. A single length of drift-net may run for two to three miles, and it is made up of many pieces of netting, each about thirty yards long and twelve yards deep, joined together end to end. The wall of netting is buoyed by floats in such a way that the top of the wall drifts a few fathoms below the surface of the sea. At night the plankton animals, on which the herrings feed, move towards the surface from deeper water, and they are followed by the herring. The fishermen therefore set their nets out at the beginning of the night and leave them drifting slowly for some hours. When a herring swims into such a wall of netting its head and perhaps an inch more of its body pass through the net, but the mesh is so designed that the rest of its body cannot pass through. The herring will then try to back out, but in so doing its gill flaps become caught by the netting and it is trapped, and unable to move either backwards or forwards. At dawn the drift nets are hauled aboard and the herrings are shaken out and taken into port.

This method of catching herrings depends to a large extent on the skill of the skipper of the drifter, who must know when and where to shoot his nets. After some experience he will get to know the appearance of the sea surface above a shoal of herrings, although it would be difficult to say how he does this. He may also notice where gannets are diving. If the dives are almost vertical the chances are that the gannets are fishing for herrings or mackerel. Nowadays, however, most drifters are fitted with echo-sounders, which will record the presence of a shoal of fish swimming beneath the ship. Here again the fish 'seen' by the echo-sounder might not be herring, but as this method becomes more and more used the skippers are getting to know the look of a herring trace as recorded by the echo-sounder, and how to distinguish it from a shoal of some other fish.

Sprats are also mid-water fish, looking rather like small herrings, and they swim in the same kind of shoal. Pilchards, which are only a little shorter than herrings but more slender in build, are caught off the coasts of Cornwall as well as further south off the western coasts of France and Portugal. Sardines are young pilchards caught by the Portuguese and tinned in olive oil. Whitebait are a mixture of young fishes, almost entirely small herring and sprat.

We may wonder how all these fish live. Much work has been done to find out the chain of food in the sea, and we can now say that the commercial fishes, and indeed all animal life in the sea, depend either directly or indirectly on the microscopic plants in the plankton. These plants are to the sea what the grass is on land. They are grazed in the first place by tiny crustaceans, not unlike the early stages of the barnacle, and by many other microscopic animals, including the young stages of starfishes, crabs and worms. In their turn these tiny animals are eaten by small fishes, which are then eaten by larger fishes. This is very roughly what happens in the open sea, and it can be drawn up as a food chain (Figure 77) which is somewhat similar to the food chain on a rocky shore. The only real difference is that in the open sea there is a greater variety of animals, including seals

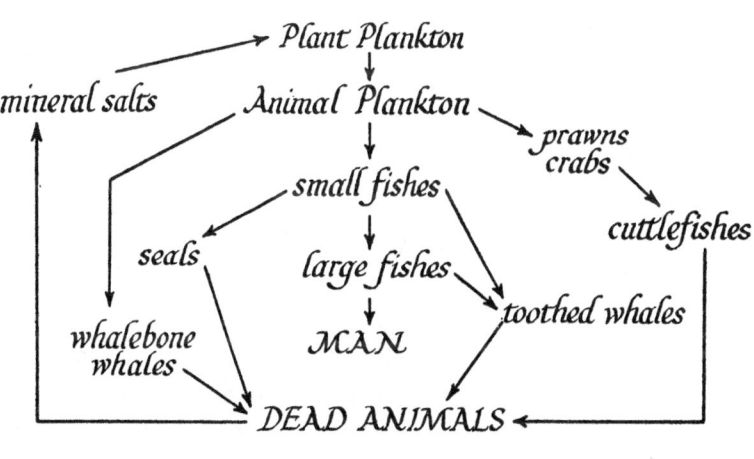

FIGURE 77

Food chain in the open sea, giving the main links. This can be compared with the food chain on a rocky shore (Figure 74)

and whales, which are not fishes, but warm-blooded mammals as we ourselves are.

Seals are fish-eaters, air-breathers, and excellent swimmers. They are often seen in coastal waters where they hunt for much of their food, and indeed they often take it ready caught from herring drift nets, much to the annoyance of the fishermen. The circus sea lion is one of this group of animals, but it does not live wild in Europe, and the ones kept here in captivity come from the coast of California. Sea lions can turn their hind limbs forwards and this allows them to do their walking and balancing tricks. True seals, on the other hand, have their hind limbs permanently turned backwards and they are not so agile on land as the sea lions. Off the coasts of Britain the common seal and the grey seal are very frequently seen. The common seal grows to about five feet in length, and is variable in colour, but usually grey-brown or dull yellow-brown. It occurs all round our coasts, especially in parts where there are sandbanks. I have often seen small herds of these seals basking in the sun on a sand-bank exposed at low tide, and on Ailsa Craig they would some-times lie out on a small jetty when there was nobody in sight.

Grey seals are larger, up to eight feet long; the colour is again variable, but always some shade of grey. They seem to have a preference for the more exposed coasts, and are common along north Cornwall, south-west Wales, and in the west of Scotland. The young grey seals are born in caves at the foot of the cliffs. These caves must make excellent protected nurseries, for they nearly always have little beaches or ledges at their inner ends where the seals can haul out of the water. Some of these caves can be reached by boat at low tide or occasionally you may need to swim into them. If you do this, never go alone, and try to carry a water-proof torch. But there are also caves whose mouths are permanently blocked by the sea. In such places the

The Sea Beyond the Shore

water may run back underground for a considerable distance, and at the inner end there may still be a little beach. To explore this type of cave would mean swimming underwater for a considerable distance. This is a job for the frogman diver who can carry his own air supply and swim beneath the water as an independent unit. Offshore diving by this method has been going on for some years in the waters off southern France and in certain parts of the United States, and there is a growing interest in it in Britain, where the newly formed Sub Aqua Club plans to do much exploration in this field.

In coastal waters the commonest of the whales, and at the same time one of the smallest is the porpoise, which travels around in 'schools', which are most interesting to watch as they swim along near the surface, at times jumping half out of the water. When they do this one can see the pale belly flashing in the sunlight. Dolphins are also small whales, similar in shape to the porpoise, but with a much sharper beak. Porpoises and dolphins, as well as pilot whales and sperm whales have teeth with which they catch and eat fishes and also cuttlefishes. The pilot whale is about twenty to thirty feet long with a blunt snout and a shiny, almost black skin; it occurs in many parts of the world but especially in the North Atlantic. In the Faeroe Islands, which lie between Iceland and the north of Scotland, pilot whales have been hunted for many hundreds of years. I once saw the Faeroe Islanders drive a school of seventy-four pilot whales ashore in a sandy bay on one of the islands. They did this from small open boats so that they ran a considerable risk from the lashing tails of the whales (Plate VIII). Once the whales were in shallow water, a party of men waded out from the shore, grappled the whales with roped hooks, and then killed them with long knives. The following day the meat and blubber were divided out according to ancient rules among those who had taken part in the hunt,

The Sea Beyond the Shore

and among the other families in the district. Before this general division the largest whale had been set aside for the man who first sighted the school, and sufficient meat had been sold to cover the cost of repairing the boats damaged during the hunt. The meat is good eating, especially when it is fresh; but much of the meat from one of these hunts has to be stored away in salt for the winter. Sperm whales are usually about sixty to seventy feet long with enormous square-built heads, with teeth each about as long as the height of this book. *Moby Dick* by Herman Melville is the story of a sperm whale. Besides being one of the best stories in the English language, it also gives an excellent picture of whale hunting in the last century.

There are, however, many whales which have no teeth. Instead they have plates of horny whalebone fringed at the edge and hanging down from the roof of the mouth. When they feed these whales take water into their mouths and the whalebone plates act as a sieve straining out the plankton from the water. The big fleshy tongue then licks the plankton from the whalebone, and starts it on its way to the stomach.

At one time whalebone whales, such as the Atlantic Right whale, were hunted in the North Atlantic by whaling ships from England and Scotland and from elsewhere in Europe. Unfortunately these slow-moving whales were hunted so much and were so easily harpooned, that they were as good as exterminated. The whaling interests then turned to the catching of the faster rorqual whales—fin whales and blue whales, and for this they have used fast whale-catchers fitted with harpoon guns. The rorquals have been hunted to a small extent in the North Atlantic and there are still two whaling stations in the Faeroes which send out catchers after them. But most of the large-scale whaling to-day is done in the Southern Ocean, in the waters fringing the Antarctic Continent. There blue whales and fin whales make up the greater part of a whaler's catch. Blue whales have been recorded up to a length of 100 feet; they are, in fact, the largest animals which have ever lived, being much heavier even than the clumsy dinosaurs and brontosaurs found as fossils. In spite of their great size they feed almost exclusively on plankton, and in Antarctic waters the most numerous animal in their food is the small crustacean, known as krill, which looks like a half-sized shrimp.

Whales are sometimes washed up on the shore, but if they are the law says that they are 'wrecks', and as such they should be reported to the Customs authorities. There is a law of Edward II, still in force, which says: '. . . the King shall have the wreck of the sea throughout the realm, whales and great sturgeons . . .'. Every few years the British Museum (Natural History) in London publishes a report on the numbers and kinds of whales stranded on the coasts of Britain. The most frequent are of porpoises, of which seventy came ashore and were reported in the years 1938-47. During the same period there were thirty-four bottle-nosed dolphins, twenty-one common dolphins and seven pilot whales, but only three sperm whales.

For years now expeditions have been sent to all parts of the world to make observations on the sea and on the animals and plants living in it. By this means enormous collections of marine animals have been gathered in from all depths and all areas, and most have been given names so that they can be accurately referred to in the future. Yet in spite of this accumulation of museum specimens we know remarkably little of how these animals behaved when alive, how they fed, moved and reproduced. Our picture of life in the open sea is tantalizingly one-sided. We know a lot about the shape of certain fishes, molluscs and so on, but we also know, mainly from remains found in whale stomachs, that there are many animals in the

The Sea Beyond the Shore

sea—some very large ones—which have never been caught and probably never seen by Man. In recent years we have read about the capture, in the Indian Ocean, of the weird coelacanth fishes —members of a group which was thought to have died out many millions of years ago. Perhaps in the years to come new fishing gear and improved methods will bring in more of these unknowns, and show that the age-long stories of sea monsters are not as wildly wrong as many would have them to be.

> *Oh what an endlesse work have I in hand,*
> *To count the sea's abundant progeny!*
> *Whose fruitfulle seede far passeth those on land*
> *And also those which wonne in th' azure sky!*
> SPENSER, *Faerie Queene,*
> Book IIII, Cant. xii, Stanza 1

Appendix of Miscellaneous Information

SEA WATER

In most areas of the ocean there are about 35 parts of salts (by weight) in every 1,000 parts of sea water. More than three-quarters of these salts consist of common salt (sodium chloride), and the remainder is made up of sulphates, carbonates, chlorides and bromides of magnesium, calcium and potassium. These are the main constituents of sea water, but there are also present in sea water minute quantities of silicon, phosphorus, nitrogen, iodine, copper and iron, as well as silver and gold. Of each of these substances there is less than one part in ten million. In fact, there are only about five parts of gold in a million million parts of sea water.

MEASUREMENTS AT SEA

1 nautical or sea mile	= 6,080 feet
1 geographical mile	= 6,086 feet
1 fathom	= 6 feet, or 1·83 metres
1 metre	= 1·09 yards, or 3·28 feet

A knot is a measurement of speed, not of length, and a speed of 1 knot = a distance travelled of 1 nautical mile per hour.

COLLECTING ON THE SHORE

For shore collecting you must first have some kind of jar to hold the animals and plants you collect. Glass jam jars or some-

Appendix of Miscellaneous Information

thing similar in size and shape will do, but they should be carried in a firm basket or box to prevent breakages. If you carry them in a haversack they will break when the haversack hits a rock, and the broken glass will be dangerous. Polythene containers are better, provided they have wide mouths.

On rocky shores a strong knife is needed for collecting limpets, barnacles and other animals and plants which are firmly fixed to the rocks. In some places we use a short steel bar as a lever to shift large stones.

On sandy shores some collectors use a garden spade, and on Penzance sands I have seen a man digging for lugworms with a long-handled Cornish shovel, but most people would probably do best with a potato fork, the kind which has flat prongs. The best net for collecting shrimps and small flatfishes from sand

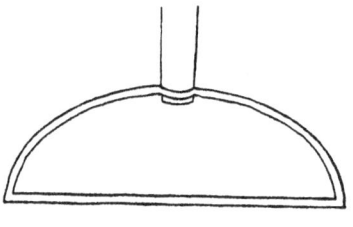

FIGURE 78
Shape of frame for a shrimp net

pools is one with a straight front edge (Figure 78), if possible bevelled so that you can push the net along the sand in front of you. For collecting prawns from large rock pools and from rocky places at low tide the frame of the net should be more pointed (Figure 79) so that you can manœuvre it into odd corners. For all net work, remember that the finer the mesh of the netting the more difficult it will be to push it or pull it through the water. Therefore always use a large mesh provided

Appendix of Miscellaneous Information

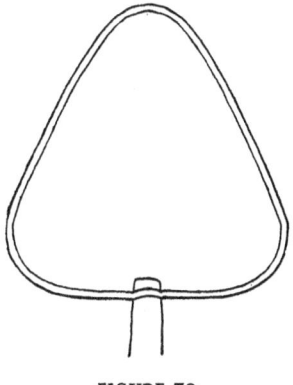

FIGURE 79

Shape of frame for a prawn net

that it will not let through those animals which you are trying to catch.

SMALL MARINE AQUARIA

Small marine aquaria are not difficult to set up and maintain provided a few simple rules are followed.

If a glass-sided tank is used the framework which holds the glass in place should be of wood, stainless steel or iron, and should never be of copper, brass, zinc, or lead. If iron is used it should be coated with a good bituminous paint to prevent rust. These glass-sided tanks are, however, expensive and I always prefer a shallow porcelain sink which you can stock as a rock pool. It is, in fact, an advantage to use shallow tanks as they expose a relatively greater area of surface to the air, so that they do not need so much artificial aeration.

The tank should be filled with real sea water. It is possible to buy 'sea salts' and dissolve them in tap water, and the resulting salty water will keep some animals such as sea anemones alive, but it may not be suitable for some of the more difficult animals such as starfishes and sea urchins. Before the aquarium is stocked with animals the tank and any stones and gravel in it should be well soaked in sea water for some days.

The water in each tank must be aerated if the depth is greater than about two inches, and this is best done with a small electric air pump which need not cost more than two to three pounds. If the water becomes cloudy there is probably a dead animal decaying in the tank and it should be removed immediately.

It is a mistake to put the larger seaweeds into marine aquaria, as they almost invariably die and foul the water. A few small green seaweeds, such as the sea lettuce, can be tried, but if the tank is placed near a north window it will soon grow its own coating of fuzzy green weed. This weed should be left to provide a supply of food for winkles and small sea urchins.

Small blennies, gobies and wrasse make excellent aquarium fish, but it is best to avoid father lashers and sea scorpions as they will eat so many of the other fish. Weevers also are unsuitable owing to their dangerous spines. Mussels are useful as their filter-feeding activities help to keep the water free from cloudiness. Sea anemones are the easiest of all marine animals to keep in an aquarium and they can be fed on finely chopped fish or meat, but avoid over-feeding them as the unconsumed portions of their rations decay very quickly.

Most shore animals will travel best in wet seaweed, but fishes should travel in water.

Living marine animals and clean sea water can be bought from the Marine Biological Association, Citadel Hill, Plymouth. Aquarium tanks and aerating pumps can be bought from most aquarists' supply shops.

PUBLIC AQUARIA

The largest aquarium in Britain is in the London Zoological

Appendix of Miscellaneous Information

Gardens, where there are three sections, marine, freshwater and tropical. The marine section contains animals from foreign waters as well as from Great Britain.

The aquaria attached to the marine biological laboratories only exhibit animals caught in home waters. These aquaria are at Plymouth (attached to the Laboratory of the Marine Biological Association of the United Kingdom), at Millport, Isle of Cumbrae, Firth of Clyde (Scottish Marine Biological Association), at the Port Erin Marine Station, Isle of Man, and at the Dove Marine Laboratory, Cullercoats, Northumberland.

There are also public aquaria at Brighton, Southsea, and Blackpool, and many other large seaside towns have a few tanks with marine animals, at any rate during the summer months.

IDENTIFICATION OF THE COMMON FLATFISHES

Based on a scheme prepared by Dr. G. A. Steven of the Plymouth Laboratory of the Marine Biological Association of the United Kingdom.

1. Lay the fish on the ground, coloured side up, and with the lower jaw and pelvic fin towards you. Then those fish which have their eyes on the right side of the head will have their heads facing to your right (Figure 34), and those with their eyes on the left side of the head will have their heads facing to your left (Figure 80), see 3 below.

2. Flatfish with eyes on the right side of the head.

(a) *Soles.* Oval in shape, small eyes. Hair-like growth on lower side of face near mouth. The Dover Sole is the commonest, but there are other soles which are caught occasionally.

(b) *Plaice Group.* Lozenge-shaped fish. Large eyes. To separate the different fish of this group, lay them on the ground, coloured side up, and gently run a finger over the

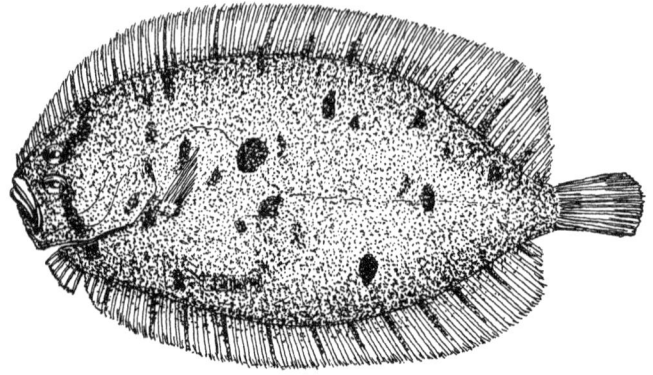

FIGURE 80

Common Top-knot, a flatfish which has the eyes on the left side of
the body, unlike the dab, flounder, plaice and sole which have them
on the right side

surface from tail to head, avoiding the lateral line up the
middle.

If the surface is rough, the fish is a dab (*Limanda limanda*)
(Figure 34). If the surface is smooth, the fish is a plaice or
flounder.

To distinguish a plaice from a flounder, run a finger from tail
to head along the line where the dorsal fin joins the body. Fish
with backward-pointing spines along the base of fin are flounders
(*Platichthys flesus*) (Figure 33).

No spines, but usually with pinkish red spots on coloured
side, plaice (*Pleuronectes platessa*).

There is one other fish of the plaice group, known as a lemon
dab or lemon sole (*Microstomus kitt*). In shape it is intermediate
between plaice and sole, it has very prominent eyes, and the
skin of the upper surface is coloured chocolate-brown, without
red spots.

Appendix of Miscellaneous Information

3. Flatfish with eyes on the left side of the head.

(a) Megrim (*Lepidorhombus whiff-iagonis*). Shaped rather like the fish of the plaice group, but very thin and bony. The eyes are large but they do not protrude much. Poor flavour.

(b) Turbot (*Scophthalmus maximus*). A thick fleshy, diamond-shaped fish; the skin covered with numerous short blunt spines. No scales. May reach a weight of 50 lb. or more.

(c) Brill (*Scophthalmus rhombus*). A thick, fleshy, oval-shaped fish; the skin has few or no blunt spines. Scales present. Not usually more than 15 lb. in weight.

SCIENTIFIC NAMES OF SOME PLANTS AND ANIMALS OF
THE SHORE AND COAST

The following lists give the scientific names of those animals and plants which have been mentioned in the text of this book. Sometimes the English name is sufficient to describe an animal or plant, but more often the English names, especially of fish, vary from district to district. In such cases the scientific name gives a more definite idea of which animal or plant is meant, and it is also international in usage.

Flowering plants

sea holly	*Eryngium maritimum*
yellow stonecrop, wall-pepper	*Sedum acre*
sea rocket	*Cakile maritima*
sea campion	*Silene maritima*
sea bindweed	*Calystegia soldanella*
sea kale	*Crambe maritima*
wild asparagus	*Asparagus officinalis*
scurvy grass	*Cochlearia officinalis*

Appendix of Miscellaneous Information

rock samphire	*Crithmum maritimum*
wild beet	*Beta vulgaris*
wild cabbage	*Brassica oleracea*
sea purslane	*Halimione portulacoides*
blue gromwell	*Lithospermum purpuro-caeruleum*
yellow horned poppy	*Glaucium flavum*
sea spurge	*Euphorbia paralias*
thrift	*Armeria maritima*
sea plantain	*Plantago maritima*
glasswort	*Salicornia*
sea blite	*Suaeda maritima*
sea aster	*Aster tripolium*
sea lavender	*Limonium vulgare*
autumn squill	*Scilla autumnalis*
carrot	*Daucus carota*
sand couch grass	*Agropyron pungens*
marram grass	*Ammophila arenaria*
eelgrass	*Zostera*

Green seaweeds

sea lettuce	*Ulva lactuca*
No English names	{ *Enteromorpha intestinalis* / *Cladophora* }

Brown seaweeds

channelled wrack	*Pelvetia canaliculata*
flat wrack	*Fucus platycarpus*
bladder wrack	*Fucus vesiculosus*
knotted wrack	*Ascophyllum nodosum*
toothed wrack	*Fucus serratus*

Appendix of Miscellaneous Information

tangle-weeds	Laminaria saccharina
	Laminaria digitata
	Laminaria cloustoni
thong weed	Himanthalia lorea
bootlace weed	Chorda filum
dabberlocks	Alaria esculenta

Red seaweeds

carragheen (Irish moss)	Chondrus crispus
'Gigartina' weed	Gigartina
dulse	Rhodymenia palmata
'Corallina' weed	Corallina officinalis
Lithophyllum ('stony-leaf')	Lithophyllum
laver	Porphyra laciniata

Mammals

common seal	Phoca vitulina
grey seal	Halichoerus grypus
porpoise	Phocæna phocæna
bottle-nosed dolphin	Tursiops truncatus
common dolphin	Delphinus delphis
pilot whale	Globicephala melæna
sperm whale	Physeter catodon
fin whale	Balænoptera physalus
blue whale	Balænoptera musculus
Atlantic Right whale	Balæna glacialis

Birds

chough	Pyrrhocorax pyrrhocorax
Herring gull	Larus argentatus
Lesser black-backed gull	Larus fuscus
Great black-backed gull	Larus marinus

common gull	*Larus canus*
kittiwake	*Rissa tridactyla*
black-headed gull	*Larus ridibundus*
common tern	*Sterna hirundo*
Arctic tern	*Sterna macrura*
great skua	*Stercorarius skua*
Arctic skua	*Stercorarius parasiticus*
Manx shearwater	*Puffinus puffinus*
fulmar	*Fulmarus glacialis*
storm petrel	*Hydrobates pelagicus*
oystercatcher	*Hæmatopus ostralegus*
ringed plover	*Charadrius hiaticula*
turnstone	*Arenaria interpres*
dunlin	*Calidris alpina*
knot	*Calidris canutus*
purple sandpiper	*Calidris maritima*
whimbrel	*Numenius phæopus*
sanderling	*Crocethia alba*
puffin	*Fratercula arctica*
razorbill	*Alca torda*
guillemot	*Uria aalge*
gamet	*Sula bassana*
shag	*Phalacrocorax aristotelis*
cormorant	*Phalacrocorax carbo*

Fishes

common dogfish	*Scyllium canicula*
thornback ray	*Raia clavata*
common skate	*Raia batis*
herring	*Clupea harengus*
sprat	*Clupe sprattus*
pilchard	*Clupea pilchardus*

Appendix of Miscellaneous Information

mackerel	*Scomber scombrus*
conger eel	*Conger vulgaris*
sea stickleback	*Spinachia vulgaris*
worm pipe-fish	*Nerophis lumbriciformis*
sand eel	*Ammodytes lanceolatus*
grey mullet	*Mugil chelo*
red mullet	*Mullus surmuletus*
cod	*Gadus morrhua*
whiting	*Gadus merlangus*
haddock	*Gadus æglefinus*
pollack	*Gadus pollachius*
hake	*Merluccius merluccius*
three-bearded rockling	*Onos tricirratus*
five-bearded rockling	*Onos mustela*
four-bearded rockling	*Onos cimbrius*
tompot blenny	*Blennius gattorugine*
shanny (smooth blenny)	*Blennius pholis*
butterfly blenny	*Blennius ocellaris*
Montagu's blenny	*Blennius galerita*
eel-pout (viviparous blenny)	*Zoarces viviparus*
butterfish or gunnel	*Centronotus gunnellus*
viper weever	*Trachinus vipera*
Cornish sucker	*Lepadogaster gouani*
rock goby	*Gobius niger*
paganelle goby	*Gobius paganellus*
two-spot goby	*Gobius flavescens*
sand goby	*Gobius minutus*
halibut	*Hippoglossus vulgaris*
sole (dover sole)	*Solea vulgaris*
plaice	*Pleuronectes platessa*
dab	*Limanda limanda*
flounder	*Platichthys flesus*

lemon dab (lemon sole)	*Microstomus kitt*
megrim	*Lepidorhombus whiff-iagonis*
turbot	*Scophthalmus maximus*
brill	*Scophthalmus rhombus*
top-knot	*Zeugopterus punctatus*
Ballan wrasse	*Labrus bergylta*
conner (corkwing wrasse)	*Crenilabrus melops*
rock wrasse (Jago's goldsinny)	*Ctenolabrus rupestris*
rock cook	*Centrolabrus exoletus*
cuckoo wrasse	*Labrus mixtus*
bass	*Morone labrax*
father lasher	*Cottus scorpius*
sea scorpion	*Cottus bubalis*
pogge	*Agonus cataphractus*
lumpsucker	*Cyclopterus lumpus*

Crustaceans

shrimp	*Crangon vulgaris*
prawn	*Leander serratus*
spiny lobster (*langouste*)	*Palinurus vulgaris*
shore crab	*Carcinus moenas*
edible crab	*Cancer pagurus*
swimming crabs	*Portunus depurator* *Portunus puber*
hermit crabs	*Eupagurus bernhardus* *Eupagurus prideauxi*
porcelain crab	*Porcellana platycheles*
sandhopper	*Talitrus saltator*
gribble	*Limnoria lignorum*
sea slater	*Ligia oceanica*
acorn barnacle	*Balanus balanoides*
goose barnacle	*Lepas anatifera*

Appendix of Miscellaneous Information

buoy-making barnacle   *Lepas fascicularis*

Molluscs

common limpet	*Patella vulgata*
blue-rayed limpet	*Patina pellucida*
common periwinkle	*Littorina littorea*
dwarf winkle	*Littorina littoralis*
top-shells	$\left\{\begin{array}{l} \textit{Gibbula cineraria} \\ \textit{Gibbula umbilicalis} \\ \textit{Calliostoma zizyphinum} \end{array}\right.$
whelk	*Buccinum undatum*
dog whelk	*Nucella (Purpura) lapillus*
netted dog whelk	*Nassarius reticulatus*
oyster	*Ostrea edulis*
mussel	*Mytilus edulis*
cockle	*Cardium edule*
razor-shell	*Ensis siliqua*
ship-worm	*Teredo navalis*
octopus	*Octopus vulgaris* and *Eledone cirrosa*
cuttlefish	*Eusepia officinalis*
coat-of-mail shell	*Acanthochitona crinitus*

Coelenterates

Portuguese Man-o'-War	*Physalia arethusa*
'by-the-wind sailor'	*Velella spirans*
beadlet sea anemone	*Actina equina*
snakelocks sea anemone	*Anemonia sulcata*
dahlia sea anemone	*Tealia felina*
common jelly fish	*Aurelia aurita*
sea-firs, such as	*Obelia* and *Sertularia*
Devon cup coral	*Caryophyllia smithi*
lucernarian	*Haliclystus auricula*

Appendix of Miscellaneous Information

Echinoderms

common starfish	*Asterias rubens*
gibbous starfish	*Asterina gibbosa*
brittle-stars, offshore	*Ophiothrix fragilis*
among Corallina weed	*Amphipholis squamata*
sea urchins	*Echinus esculentus*
	Psammechinus miliaris
heart urchin	*Echinocardium cordatum*
sea cucumber	*Cucumaria saxicola*

Worms

sand mason	*Lanice conchilega*
peacock fan worm	*Sabella pavonina*
lugworm	*Arenicola marina*
ragworm	*Perinereis cultrifera*
Spirorbis worm	*Spirorbis borealis*

Ascidians

sea squirts, many species	*Ciona intestinalis*
such as	*Ascidiella aspersa*

Sponges

purse sponge	*Grantia compressa*
breadcrumb sponge	*Halichondria panicea*

A List of Books to Read

GENERAL BOOKS ON THE SEA AND COASTLINE

RUSSELL, F. S. AND YONGE, C. M. *The Seas* (Warne, 2nd edition 1936).

COLMAN, JOHN S., *The Sea and its Mysteries* (Bell, 1950).

STEERS, J. A., *The Sea Coast* (New Naturalist Series, Collins, 1953).

SEASHORE

YONGE, C. M., *The Seashore* (New Naturalist Series, Collins, 1949). A very comprehensive book on the seashore between tides, illustrated by colour and black and white photographs by D. P. Wilson and others.

WILSON, D. P., *Life of the Shore and Shallow Sea* (Nicholson & Watson, 1935). Illustrated by the author's own excellent photographs, this book deals with the life of the offshore waters as well as that of the tidal zone.

WILSON, D. P., *They Live in the Sea* (Collins, 1947). A collection of photographs with descriptive texts.

HEPBURN, IAN, *Flowers of the Coast* (New Naturalist Series, Collins, 1953).

NEWBIGIN, M., *Life by the Seashore*, revised by R. Elmhirst (Allen & Unwin, 1931).

EALES, N. B., *The Littoral Fauna of Great Britain* (Cambridge University Press, 2nd edition, 1950).

JOHNS, C. A., *Flowers of the Field*, revised by R. B. Blakelock (Routledge & Kegan Paul, 1948).

A List of Books to Read

FISHES

NORMAN, J. R., *A History of Fishes* (Benn, 1947).

ROULE, L., *Fishes: their Ways of Life* (Routledge, 1935).

WHALES

NORMAN, J. R., AND FRASER, F. C., *Giant Fishes, Whales and Dolphins* (Putnam, 1948).

MELVILLE, HERMANN, *Moby Dick, or the White Whale* (available in the Everyman Library: Dent).

SEA BIRDS

JOHNS, C. A., *British Birds and their Haunts*, revised by W. B. Alexander (Routledge and Kegan Paul, 1948).

FISHER, JAMES, *Bird Recognition*, Vol. I (Penguin Books, Harmondsworth, Middlesex, 1947). This and the next book are the best and most convenient guides to the identification of sea birds and waders.

FITTER, R. S. R., *Pocket Guide to British Birds* (Collins, 1953).

FISHER, JAMES, *The Fulmar* (New Naturalist Monograph, Collins, 1953).

LOCKLEY, R. M., *Shearwaters* (Dent, 1942).

FISHER, JAMES, AND LOCKLEY, R. M., *Sea Birds* (New Naturalist Series, Collins, 1954).

MARINE AQUARIA

KNOWLES, F. G. W., *Freshwater and Salt-water Aquaria* (Harrap, 1953). This is the best modern book on the maintenance of small marine aquaria.

Index

(Page numbers in italic refer to pages containing a text figure.)

Index

Index

Index

Index

Index

For Product Safety Concerns and Information please contact our EU
representative GPSR@taylorandfrancis.com
Taylor & Francis Verlag GmbH, Kaufingerstraße 24, 80331 München, Germany

www.ingramcontent.com/pod-product-compliance
Lightning Source LLC
Chambersburg PA
CBHW070545100726
47907CB00004B/1274

* 9 7 8 1 0 3 2 7 7 6 1 7 0 *